Revolution and Terror in France 1789-1795

D.G. Wright

Senior Lecturer in History
Huddersfield Polytechnic

LONGMAN

Longman
1724-1974

LONGMAN GROUP LIMITED
London

*Associated companies, branches
and representatives throughout the world*

First published 1974

ISBN 0 582 35209 6

Printed in Great Britain
by Whitstable Litho, Whitstable, Kent

For Simon

Contents

Part Four · Assessment

Part Five · Documents

Introduction to the Series

The seminar method of teaching is being used increasingly. It is a way of learning in smaller groups through discussion, designed both to get away from and to supplement the basic lecture techniques. To be successful, the members of a seminar must be informed—or else, in the unkind phrase of a cynic—it can be a 'pooling of ignorance'. The chapter in the textbook of English or European history by its nature cannot provide material in this depth, but at the same time the full academic work may be too long and perhaps too advanced.

For this reason we have invited practising teachers to contribute short studies on specialised aspects of British and European history with these special needs in mind.

For this series the authors have been asked to provide, in addition to their basic analysis, a full selection of documentary material of all kinds and an up-to-date and comprehensive bibliography. Both these sections are referred to in the text, but it is hoped that they will prove to be valuable teaching and learning aids in themselves.

Note on the System of References:
A bold number in round brackets (**5**) in the text refers the reader to the corresponding entry in the Bibliography section at the end of the book. A bold number in square brackets, preceded by 'doc' [**docs 6, 8**] refers the reader to the corresponding items in the section of Documents, which follows the main text.

PATRICK RICHARDSON
General Editor

Acknowledgements

We are grateful to the following for permission to reproduce copyright material:
Ginn & Company Limited for an extract from *The Press in the French Revolution* (1971) by J. Gilchrist and W.J. Murray and to The John Rylands University Library of Manchester for *Rylands French MS. 51. fols. 15r-16v.*

The author wishes to thank Miss Susan Roberts for typing the manuscript.
The cover is reproduced by permission of Collection Viollet.

PART ONE

Introduction

. . . mais la conduite des hommes dépend toujours d'un grand nombre de facteurs, et c'est pourquoi l'histoire est la plus difficile et la moins avancée des disciplines d'observation.

Georges Lefebvre
Sur la Loi du 22 Prairial An II (1951)

1 The Problem

No student of modern history can ignore the French Revolution. Like the Renaissance, the seventeenth-century crisis and war and revolution in 1914-19, it marks a geological fault in the strata of modern history. Knowledge of it is essential for any understanding of the development of the modern world. In the words of Professor R.R. Palmer, the French Revolution constitutes 'the great turning point of modern civilisation' (52, introduction). It was the Revolution which launched the assault on nobility, privilege, servitude, tithes and feudal dues. It was the Revolution which spread the ideas of national sovereignty, national self-determination, individual rights and the rule of law. The greatest twentieth-century historian of the French Revolution saw its essence as the question of equality, without which liberty would remain the prerogative of the few: *'Avant tout, elle fut la Révolution de l'égalité'* (7). Europe was never the same after 1789, for the Revolution began fundamental changes in government, an increase in the nature and scale of warfare, and a challenge to the old hierarchy, institutions and culture of the *ancien régime*. Classes, status groups and parties pushed kings, nobles and bishops over to the defensive (66). On 20 September 1792 the French army defeated the Prussians at Valmy. Goethe, who was present in the Prussian camp, told his dejected companions: 'From this place and from this day forth commences a new era in the world's history, and you can all say that you were present at its birth.' The threat which the revolution in arms presented to the established European social order made a return to the *ancien régime* impossible in the long run. Modern Europe may be dated from the cannonade at Valmy.

The French Revolution is riddled with paradoxes. The concern with individual liberty and the increased participation of the people in government existed alongside the consolidation of the centralised modern state and the dictatorship of 1793-94. A concern with humanitarianism, exemplified by the abolition of torture and replacement of the horrors of breaking on the wheel by the relatively humane guillotine, coexisted with a new tradition of public violence and insurrection. Enthusiasm for individual political rights was blended with a new emphasis on the rights of property. The slogan of universal brotherhood was followed by intense nationalism. Before 1792 revolutionaries denounced war as a stratagem of kings and aristocrats: after 1792 conscription for the 'wars of liberty' foreshadowed the ordeal of total war and the reversion to barbarism depicted in the searing war paintings of Goya. The Revolution retarded French industrial and commercial development in the short run, but ultimately replaced the regulated, mercantilist tariff economy by a free national market which was to open the way to modern capitalist economic growth in the nineteenth century. Moreover, it was the revolutionary period which saw the beginnings of the socialism which was later to attack capitalism.

Students may be forgiven if they approach the study of the French Revolution with some trepidation. So much seems to happen in the relatively short period between 1789 and 1795, while its interpretation still bristles with controversy. There seems little agreement on what exactly *was* the French Revolution. Indeed, Alfred Cobban questioned whether there was a revolution at all: 'The real fallacy behind all the myths of the French Revolution – the idea that there was *a* French Revolution, which you can be for or against' (**29**, ch. **5**). If there *was* a French Revolution, just when did it begin and end? What precisely were its causes and consequences? Can it be described as a 'bourgeois revolution', a 'democratic revolution', or a 'revolution for equality'? Was there in fact one Revolution, or were there several? Who, for that matter, were the revolutionaries, who have tended to be described as part of such faceless and anonymous abstractions as 'the peasants', 'the bourgeoisie', 'the Paris mob' and so on, categories which seem to appear and disappear at various stages of the Revolution in somewhat puzzling fashion, like the Cheshire Cat in *Alice in Wonderland?*

Historians disagree about almost any historical problem. The higher the level of historical studies, the fewer 'right answers' there are to provide a sense of neatness and security. No problem has provoked more controversy than the origins, nature and consequences of the French Revolution. It is an inexhaustible subject. More has been written about it than about anything else in history, whilst the flood of books and articles shows no signs of abating. Such disagreement goes back to the period itself, when deep and bitter divisions were sown among men throughout the West. As well as a Revolution, there was the Counter-Revolution, both inside and outside France. Supporters of the Counter-Revolution – the aristocracy, the Church plus substantial numbers of businessmen, peasants and the very poor – were the victims of Terror and repression. But they were not annihilated. Violence against them deepened their enmity and resentment against the Revolution and all it stood for.

The division between Frenchmen at the end of the eighteenth century - for or against the great events of 1789 and 1793 - persisted in the nineteenth and twentieth centuries. Revolutions in France in 1830, 1848 and 1870 made the Revolution a continuing movement. Fears of a return to the 'horrors of 1793', or, alternatively, a desire to recreate the days of liberty, fraternity, democracy and cheap bread remained dominant themes in French public life. Even villages could be split between those who regarded 1789 as the unleashing of the forces of Satan, darkness and anarchy; and those who looked back on the Revolution as the dawn of liberty and enlightened rationalism, the death of privilege, inequality and superstition. As late as the 1940s, the Terror of the Year II was recalled with dread in parts of the French countryside, as the ghost of Robespierre seemed to walk behind requisitioning and rationing officials, tax collectors and anticlericals. These cleavages among Frenchmen were sustained by the growth of socialism and the impact of the Russian Revolution. If the Revolution had inspired liberals and republicans in the nineteenth century, it inspired the socialist Left in the twentieth. The former tended to look to the liberal Revolution of 1789-92; the latter to the Revolution of 1793-95, when a revolutionary dictatorship struggled against war, counter-revolution and the demands of its own supporters for direct democracy.

The debate on the French Revolution has not yet completely passed from politics into history. Lecturing at the Sorbonne in 1939, a few weeks before the outbreak of the Second World War and the collapse of the demoralised Third Republic, Georges Lefebvre this time put the emphasis on liberty as the core of the Revolution:

> Liberty supposes application, perpetual effort, strict government of self, sacrifice in contingencies, civic and private virtues. It is therefore more difficult to live as a free man than to live as a slave, and that is why men so often renounce their freedom; for freedom is in its way an invitation to a life of courage, and sometimes of heroism, as the freedom of the Christian is an invitation to a life of sainthood (52, conclusion).

Published as *Quatre-vingt-neuf*, eight thousand copies of Lefebvre's lectures were destroyed by the Vichy régime during the war.

The questions which have dominated histories of the French Revolution are those which were asked by contemporaries and by those who wrote with such passion in the nineteenth century. Was the *ancien régime* so worm-eaten that the French Revolution was 'necessary' and therefore commendable? Was the Revolution completely necessary or did it at some stage become 'excessive'? If the latter, then when did the excesses begin: with the September Massacres, the declaration of a Republic, the execution of the king, the Terror of 1793-94, or when? Can one, as Cobban asked, still see the Revolution as a monolithic *bloc*, to be either praised or condemned? How far was the Terror implicit in the ideas and events of 1789? Or was it something arbitrarily imposed by the bitter circumstances of war, counter-revolution and the impending breakdown of government?

Such fundamental questions cannot be fully answered in a short book; indeed, they probably will never produce final answers, for each generation sees the past through different eyes and answers themselves provoke further questions. The aims of this book are more modest. First, to encourage thinking about some of the problems of historical study raised by the French Revolution; second, to direct students to the work of historians of the Revolution, whose writings have been so unashamedly plundered in the following pages; and finally to examine a fraction of the mass of documentary evidence on which historians have based their judgments.

2 Revolution, Terror and the Historians

PARTISANS

Historians of the Revolution began writing during the Revolutionary period itself. Edmund Burke's *Reflections on the Revolution in France* (**1790**) damned the Revolution and all its works in emotional prose; French rejoinders were no more scholarly and much less readable. *Émigrés* after 1791 published episodic writings which stressed the role of ideas in causing the Revolution, which became a conspiracy of Freemasons, freethinkers and discontented intellectuals who plotted in their clubs and *sociétés de pensée* to overthrow the old order. Such conspirators were partly motivated by their personal desire for riches and office. Early conservative writers like Chateaubriand and de Maistre saw the Terror and 'anarchy' as the essence of the Revolution; revolutionary governments from 1792 to 1794 were unanimously condemned, while the common people received only contempt. The 'brutish and hellish' Jacobins were only slightly redeemed by their patriotism and efforts to ensure victory for French arms.

Thiers (**1823-27**) and Mignet (**1824**) were liberals who used history as a political weapon against the restored Bourbon monarchy. They saw the Revolution as a natural stage in the 'destiny' of France, pioneering liberalism and constitutionalism between 1789 and 1791 before taking a wrong turning along the road leading to Terror and dictatorship. The Revolution they exalted was that of the Third Estate, defined by them as the intellectuals and propertied middle classes who carried through the bourgeois revolution and ultimately created the France depicted in the novels of Balzac; a France which was to reassert itself in the July Revolution of 1830 (**28,30**). Jules Michelet, whose history of the Revolution appeared between 1847 and 1853, was a man of persuasive literary gifts and an intense poetical imagination. His history was written as a gospel of faith in the liberal tradition. Imbued with the spirit of the republican democrats of 1848, he was the first historian to put the common people at the centre of the Revolutionary stage. For him, the French Revolution emerged from the hunger and oppression of the masses, as well as from the idealism of all those who embraced the new ideas of liberty, justice and national sovereignty. The Revolution

7

before 1793 was the work of the whole people: the collective incarnation of virtue. The Terror, on the other hand, was the work of a wayward minority. Michelet took the study of the Revolution a stage further in two respects. First, his imagination led him to sympathise with *sans culottes* and Revolutionary leaders and to try to write 'from the inside', though he remained unaware of the diversity of the broad Revolutionary groups and the conflict between them. Secondly, he used archival sources on a greater scale than his predecessors, although his approach remained essentially literary and eschewed scholarly references.

Thomas Carlyle was outside the French liberal republican tradition, but his book on the Revolution (1837) had similarities with that of Michelet. He also wrote with passion and had deep sympathy with the *sans culottes,* though he was more of a prophet than a poet. Like Michelet, he grasped the tragedy of the revolutionary experience, but through the eyes of disillusioned Scots radicalism, Old Testament Calvinism and romantic German philosophy. He was also strongly influenced by unrest in England during the 1830s. For Carlyle, a corrupt and decadent *ancien régime* suffered the inevitable retribution of divine justice in a Revolution of chaos and destruction, where men were, like flies, the sport of the gods (29, ch. 12).

As difficult to classify is the work of Alexis de Tocqueville, whose *L'Ancien régime et la Révolution* appeared in 1856. Perhaps the most intelligent of all historians of the Revolution and still well worth reading, Tocqueville was an aristocratic liberal, disillusioned with the results of the Revolution of 1848 and the reign of Napoleon III, but nevertheless more objective than his predecessors. He saw the Revolution as the result of the irresponsible policies of an unstable monarchy in a book which was more analytical than the essentially narrative work of Thiers, Mignet and Michelet. Tocqueville wrote: 'I speak of classes, they alone must be the substance of history' and stimulated later historians of the Left to study class tension and conflict as one of the basic forces of the Revolution. But he also influenced the Right, first by his unwillingness to condemn the *ancien régime* as a whole, though he admitted it could not survive without major reforms, and secondly by his argument that the Revolution emerged, not from a state of misery and economic stagnation, but from years of prosperity and rising expectations, culminating in a situation rendered intolerable by class antagonisms and ambitions. Tocqueville had little sympathy with the common people, seeing the essential achievement of the Revolution as not so much the extension of liberty, but the creation of a strong, centralised administrative machine, which prepared the way for Napoleonic rule and the replacement of one despotism by another.

The conservative tradition of the Right was revived by Hippolyte Taine, whose first volume on the Revolution was published in 1876. Like Tocqueville, Taine was a disillusioned liberal, unnerved by the Paris Commune of 1871. His disillusion sank so deep that it emerged as a savage, passionate frenzy. A brilliant stylist, who wrote with overpowering emotional force, Taine depended as much on his own brand of social psychology as on historical documentation. For him, the Revolution marked the dissolution of an exhausted social order, poisoned by the 'morbid germ' of the doctrine of the sovereignty of the people. The revolutionary crowds were neither Michelet's admirable engine of the Revolution nor Carlyle's pitiable wretches, but 'scum' and 'rabble', motivated by base desires for blood and loot. Those who attacked the Bastille on 14 July 1789 were 'bandits' and 'vagabonds'. Revolutionary leaders were dismissed as eccentric and dogmatic refugees from the prosperous bourgeoisie, men for whom the Revolution provided an opportunity to put into practice their fanatical and half-baked ideas, with the disastrous consequence of anarchy and mob rule.

SCHOLARS

Michelet used newly available archival documents, as did the socialist historian Louis Blanc, who also provided footnote references. Tocqueville's sources included a mass of documents in the Archives Nationales, the departmental archives of Indre-et-Loire and registers of communes and, lastly, *cahiers*. Nevertheless, the age of scrupulous and exact Revolutionary historical scholarship, based on the critical methods of Ranke and the German school of historians, began only with the work of Alphonse Aulard (1849-1928), who in 1886 became the first occupant of the chair of the history of the Revolution established at the Sorbonne by the French government and the city of Paris. Although he aimed at careful and systematic use of primary sources, Aulard was a fervent radical, anticlerical apologist for the early years of the Third Republic, who saw the Revolution primarily in political and ideological terms. According to Aulard, the enlightened ideas and principles of national sovereignty put forward by peaceable and sensible men in 1789 led naturally to democracy, republicanism and anticlericalism. Violence and materialism were largely the preserve of the aristocracy and the nonjuring clergy. Unlike his liberal predecessors, Aulard saw the main Revolution taking place after 1792, when France became a republic under the heroic leadership of Danton. The Revolution of 1789-91, on the other hand, was really government by men afraid of the people and therefore unwilling to take revolutionary principles to their logical conclusion (15, part iii).

The new scholarly approach to Revolutionary studies was outlined in Aulard's instructions to his pupils: be rigorously objective and scientific; use the procedures developed by philologists and the German historians; always draw from the sources and say nothing without supplying documentary evidence; give precise references, whilst presenting the facts 'in an impartial and objective manner'. Besides numerous books, Aulard and his assistants published a wide range of documents on social and economic life and the activities of the Committee of Public Safety. Thus Revolutionary history became established as a 'scientific' discipline in the universities, as well as retaining its place in the literary Academy and on the political battlefield.

The Radical monopoly in the universities was challenged in the early 1900s by Augustin Cochin, a pupil of the *École des Chartres* who defended the views of Taine and the conservatives. A devout Catholic, Cochin argued that the Revolution had basically ideological causes, being the result of a campaign to destroy the monarchy and the Church by intellectuals inspired with the subversive ideas of the Enlightenment. Seizing the old 'conspiracy thesis' of the early *émigrés* and skilfully refurbishing it, he condemned the Revolution without reservation. Masonic lodges, political clubs and the thousands of miscellaneous associations that made up the *sociétés de pensée* formed, according to Cochin, a network for the propagation of revolutionary doctrines and the hatching of plans to destroy the social order. Cochin's approach was followed by literary historians, whose scholarship was less than his, and less than that of the historians of the Left. Louis Madelin was a Bonapartist whose book on the Revolution in 1911 condemned the *ancien régime* and approved of the aims of the Third Estate, but saw the Revolution as going wrong as early as August 1789, speedily dissolving into anarchy, demagoguery and mob rule. Napoleon eventually came to the rescue and imposed order and sanity. Books on the Revolution by Pierre Gaxotte in 1928 and Frantz Funck-Brentano in 1926 were influenced by their horror of the Russian Revolution of 1917 and the subsequent 'Bolshevik danger'. The latter were seen as the heirs of the 'anarchists' of the Terror of 1793-94. These books, which owed a lot to Taine, made up in readability what they lacked in scholarship and gained a wide circulation in the inglorious final days of the Third Republic among Frenchmen who were afraid of socialism and communism and were eager for easy explanations and a patriotic and picturesque past (27).

Until the early years of the twentieth century, historians of both Right and Left tended to see the French Revolution 'from above', that is, from the point of view of Paris and the central government. Peasants and *sans culottes* tended to appear only in the guise of mindless automata in the grip of either Revolutionary leaders or inexorable historical forces. At the turn of the century, however, historians became increasingly influenced by Marxist ideas, which have dominated scholarly writing on the Revolution until very recently. Such influence involved a move from studying political events and leaders towards social and economic questions; a change of direction which led to looking at the Revolution 'from below', that is from the point of view of the interests and pre-occupations of the common people. The new point of view implied interpreting the Revolution as more of a class struggle than a mere conflict of ideas and doctrines.

This socialist approach was not in fact entirely new, since it harked back to the writing of Buonarotti and Louis Blanc. It was, however, pioneered in scholarly fashion by Jean Jaurès **(1862-1914)**, a philosopher, politician and socialist leader whose great intellectual gifts were tempered by an admirable tolerance, humility and compassion, as well as a lack of the bellicose nationalism which has tainted so much French historical writing. In the introduction to the first volume of his *Histoire socialiste de la Révolution française* **(1901)** he complained that historians had suffered from the 'bourgeois illusion' that the Revolution was mainly a political one, and therefore neglected social issues, questions of economic development and the class struggle. Jaurès began a new approach by looking closely at the *sans culottes* and at divisions within the Revolutionary Assemblies, as well as looking at the Revolution in the provinces, though he never neglected the importance of ideas.

Albert Mathiez **(1874-1932)** proved to be the greatest disciple of Jaurès. In fact he was a pupil of Aulard who turned against his master, adopted a Marxist interpretation and saw Robespierre rather than Danton as the hero of the Revolution. A ruthless professional, who wrote with great force and clarity and worked himself to death in the archives, Mathiez saw the incompetence and scandals of the pre-1914 years as evidence of the bankruptcy of the liberal and anticlerical tradition. The Russian Revolution and the experience of economic control during the First World War led him to focus on social and economic factors during the Revolution, especially the problem of food supplies and the Maximum **(32)**. Mathiez's view of the Terror was that of the 'thesis of circumstances'; that is of a Revolutionary government adopting almost socialist policies under the pressure of war, counter-revolution, social conflict and economic crisis, rather than because of a slavish obedience to Rousseauist ideology. Mathiez also undermined the old picture of the Revolution as a single bloc, arguing that there were several revolutions, including the aristocratic revolt of 1787-88 **(28,30,31)**.

The greatest academic historian of the French Revolution was Georges Lefebvre **(1874-1959)**, who like Mathiez, regarded Jaurès as his master. An austere Republican from Lille, Lefebvre called himself a Guesde Marxist and set much of his work within a Marxist framework, though it kept breaking the bounds. For him the Revolution was about liberty and equality. It also marked the rise of the bourgeoisie to dominance of French and European society. Yet Lefebvre had much in common with the liberal school of French historians, not least his rationalism, his hatred of the nobility and privilege and his intense pride in being French. His boundless curiosity and immense enthusiasm for research remained undimmed until his death at eighty-five, while his command of a wide range of sources is never likely to be surpassed.

Lefebvre asked new questions and opened up areas of Revolutionary history which are still being explored. A pioneer of social and economic history, he was writing before 1914 on the grain trade, the problems of food supply, price controls and the Maximum. He realised that the *problème des subsistances* was crucial to all French governments between the seventeenth century and the 1820s and that questions of public order were closely linked to this matter of the distribution of grain. At a time when Aulard and Mathiez were still preoccupied with political and religious questions, Lefebvre published a seminal collection of documents on the Revolutionary food supply. His vast and erudite thesis on the northern peasants in 1924 was the model for the new social history which has come to dominate Revolutionary studies. It showed that the peasantry was not composed of superstitious rural idiots who blithely followed directions of nobles and parish priests. On the contrary, the peasantry was composed of widely differing social groups whose interests frequently conflicted, though these groups were capable of acting in relative unison, without direction from above, in the summer of 1789. Proud of his own provincial origins and originally trained as a geographer, Lefebvre was always aware of the complicated role of the provinces during the Revolution and of the importance of regional differences. At the time of his death he was writing a social and economic study of the Orléanais, published posthumously **(47)**.

A further original contribution of Lefebvre was his writing on 'collective mentalities'. His work on the peasantry taught him much about the nature and operation of the popular mind and made him realise that what people *thought* was happening was often as important, or even more important, than what actually *was* happening. Lefebvre used the new disciplines of sociology and social psychology to help to explain the influence of rumour, panic and the fear of 'plots' at various key stages of the Revolution. His study of *La Grande Peur* **(1932)** of the summer of

1789 brought a new dimension to the history of the Revolution. He was very much the complete historian, for he also wrote about foreign trade, currency questions and the role of political factions in 1793-94, as well as publishing what is still the best book on Napoleon.

Lefebvre was the last great master to dominate Revolutionary studies. He left no school of disciples, as had Aulard and Mathiez, and saw some of his most distinguished pupils go off into new areas of research, though they followed him in studying the Revolution from below. Albert Soboul, a somewhat stricter Marxist than Lefebvre himself, published a massive thesis on the Parisian *sans culottes* in 1958 **(102)**. He analysed the political structure of popular Parisian institutions and revealed the 'mentality' and attitudes of the *sans culottes* for the first time, rescuing them from the slanders of Taine and the conservative school. George Rudé, an Englishman who also writes from a Marxist viewpoint, undertook a similar task for the crowds involved in the great *journées* in Paris during the Revolution and showed that the 'Paris mob' is a misnomer **(71)**. Richard Cobb, another Englishman, published a vast thesis on the *armées révolutionnaires* in 1961-63, illuminating the nature of the Terror in the Paris region and the provinces and throwing new light on the vexed question of dechristianisation **(104)**.

The last powerful manifestation of the traditional conservative approach was *The Origins of Totalitarian Democracy*, published by the Hebrew scholar J.L. Talmon in 1952 **(167)**. This book had influence far beyond the circle of scholars to whom it was primarily addressed and amongst whom it made little impression. Partly inspired by Tocqueville, Talmon argued that radical all-embracing philosophies tend to lead to the suppression of individual freedom. Eighteenth-century thinkers began a process which ended by undermining liberal values. The ideas of Rousseau in particular, it was alleged, marked the origins of Revolutionary dictatorship and totalitarianism in the modern world.

During the last twenty years or so much of the old polemic on the French Revolution has faded away. Despite the rather crude Marxism of some of his occasional writings, Lefebvre's research showed that the French Revolution as a total phenomenon with a unity of its own, to be praised or condemned, is a false perspective. Rather than a single Revolution, there were a series of revolutions: the noble revolt of 1787-88, the liberal revolution of 1789-91, the popular revolution of 1792-94, the reaction of 1795-99 and the Bonapartist revolution which followed. In any case, there is a depth of research where ideology becomes largely irrelevant. Paradoxically, much work undertaken by Marxists has made the old Marxist model of the French Revolution, with its stereotyped vocabulary, increasingly inadequate for an understanding of the revolutionary period. Moreover, experience of wars and revolution in the twentieth century has deepened our understanding of the kind of pressure to which France was subjected at the end of the eighteenth century. Research in departmental and local archives has revealed the dangers of seeing any close similarity between French society in the Revolutionary period and Western society of a later industrial age.

Historians of the Left are now willing to admit that peasants and workers had no political programme or class consciousness akin to that of later urban industrial workers. Nor does the concept of the third estate and National Assembly as a bourgeoisie, aiming at the expansion of industrial capitalism, survive recent research. No longer can the Revolution be seen in terms of a simple class structure, for research has revealed not only the interaction and interdependence of particular social groups, but also the internal divisions within those groups. The Terror is no longer seen simply as either the unleashing by dogmatic megalomaniacs of a bloodthirsty and covetous mob, or as a time when honest men, inspired by classical virtues, took the opportunity to clear privilege, corruption and frivolity from the face of France. Like the Revolution itself, the Terror was not a monolith. It was to some extent a class war; it was certainly a conflict, or rather a series of conflicts, based on rival ideologies and personal rivalries and jealousies; it was partly an attempt to reduce large-scale unorganised and unofficial violence by substituting official violence on a more restricted scale. The 'thesis of circumstances' still holds; for war, counter-revolution and the continuing fear of an 'aristocratic plot' imposed, with ruthless logic, the sanctions of a war economy, the necessity of 'national defence' and the assumption that those who were not enthusiastic for the Revolution were against it.

Meanwhile further research among the vast range of primary sources continues to modify our view of the Revolution and its place in the history of France and Europe. Professor Labrousse and his pupils have studied in great detail economic conditions and the social structure in France on the eve of the Revolution. Statistical and computer techniques have been used to analyse notarial archives, such as wills, marriage contracts and transfers of property, as well as fiscal records. Such research has shown the inadequacy of such blanket terms as *noblesse, bourgeois, ouvrier* and *paysan* to describe a society as complex as that of eighteenth-century France **(98)**.

The vast resources of the French departmental archives are now being systematically tapped. Much research is being undertaken on provincial France, particularly with regard to the operation of the Terror outside Paris **(129-135)**. Such studies have brought to the fore the neglected importance of the Counter-Revolution, regarded by traditional liberal historians as an aberration hardly worth discussing, but knowledge of which is essential for any understanding of either the Terror or the European conflict of ideas and armies which the Revolution provoked **(90-95; 118-122)**. Study of the Counter-Revolution and the White Terror has led to renewed interest in the neglected period after 1794, now seen as the natural sequel to what went before, rather than as a somewhat bizarre and uninteresting contradiction. From a rather different angle, the writings of Jacques Godechot and R.R. Palmer on the 'Atlantic Revolution' have placed the French Revolution more firmly in its international context **(14, 15, 16)**. Revolutionary history is therefore being transformed. 'Spreading out from the history of the Revolution', wrote Alfred Cobban, 'one can envisage a reshaping of modern French history which will transcend the arbitrary political cleavages of the past, and indeed throw light on the whole history of the modern world' **(33**, ch. 13**)**.

PART TWO

The First
French Revolution

3   Pre-Revolution 1787-89

THE CRISIS OF THE *ANCIEN RÉGIME*

The French Revolution, which began with the aristocratic revolt of 1788 and came to a head in the popular revolt of 1789, can be seen as part of a general movement in the western world which continued after 1789 for at least a decade and affected almost all countries in Europe west of the Urals and north of the Pyrenees. In both Europe and America, rulers and sections of the ruled were in conflict. This broad movement can be seen as an 'Atlantic' or 'Democratic' revolution, if one accepts the arguments of Jacques Godechot and R.R. Palmer (**14, 15, 16**). Besides the American Revolution of 1773-83, there were movements all over Europe which aimed at challenging the traditions, privileges, institutions and loyalties of aristocratic society. In Geneva, England and Holland there was growing dissatisfaction with established forms of social stratification and an increasing unwillingness to accept the control of government and public office by privileged and self-recruiting groups (**14**, vol. i, ch. 1).

Compared with the French Revolution, however, these European movements were limited in scope. Conflict tended to be between aristocratic rulers who sought to modernise the machinery of government and privileged nobles who opposed them in defence of traditional interests and localised society (**26**, ch.2). Even in republics like Geneva and the Netherlands, the struggle was largely confined to groups of wealthy patricians. Everywhere the conflict involved minorities of the population rather than the urban and peasant masses. In the long run they achieved relatively little, for they resembled a salvo of musket fire which emitted much noise and smoke, but did little to shake the basic structure of the fortress of society. Only in France in 1789 did the heavy artillery fire of a popular revolution create a barrage so intense that the fortress crumbled. Not only were government institutions overthrown, but the social order itself was also blasted and transformed. The French Revolution was more violent, more radical, more prolonged and more democratic than its predecessors. No other revolution involved such widespread participation by the peasants and urban common people. The fact that revolts in Europe were frequent after 1789 and that Europe was plunged into warfare of a new intensity and scale between 1792 and

1815 bears testimony to the power of the French Revolution as the pre-
dominant element in the European revolutionary mixture (9, ch. 2; 14,
vol. ii; 16).

The demographic, social, economic and ideological pressures which
provoked a general crisis of the *ancien régime* in the West were felt most
intensely in France, where conflict was endemic since the 1760s.
Population increase was accompanied by the fragmentation of peasant
holdings, inadequate increases in agricultural productivity and bad
harvests after 1770. Both wages and the level of employment lagged
behind the rising price of grain and other basic necessities. Hence substantial sections of the French population were faced with a declining
standard of living, while the whole country faced a major economic
crisis in the 1780s (44; 15 part ii, ch.2; 68). In Strasbourg, for example
rapid population growth meant that by 1789 there was a deficit of
20,000 sacks of grain compared with supplies in 1743. The result was
death, emigration and an increasing horde of paupers, beggars and
vagrants (56).

French agriculture and industry were both backward compared with
England. Whilst generalisation about French society under the *ancien
régime* is dangerous, for regional variations were enormous, there is little
doubt that payment of tithes to the Church and feudal dues to the
nobility weighed heavily on the peasant proprietors, who owned about
a third of the land of France, mostly in the poorer and more remote
regions. It is also evident that population pressure and price increases
meant a rise in the numbers of the rural proletariat: those who owned
no land and who, in bad years, were driven into smuggling, vagrancy and
banditry [doc. 1]. If all groups of peasants agreed that the burdens of the
ancien régime on their land – the bulk of government taxation, tithes
and feudal dues – were too heavy in a deteriorating economic situation,
then there still remained the fact that rural society was split and plagued
with antagonisms in the 1770s and 1780s. Only large farmers and richer
peasant proprietors advocated new methods like enclosure and crop
rotation; the mass of the peasantry was opposed to such 'agrarian
individualism' (68, 52, 31, ch. 9; 40, ch. 3; 67).

Machine factories and large-scale industrial capitalism were rare in
France. The domestic system dominated rural industry and the small
workshop that of the towns. Places like Elbeuf, the wool-textile centre
of Normandy which had virtually no nobles and was controlled by a
rising industrial middle class, with 59.7 per cent of its population wage-
earners in 1785, were very exceptional (50, chs 1 and 2). Most towns
were either agrarian market towns, great ports, or ecclesiastical and
administrative centres. Here, as in the countryside, society was finely

graded and inequalities were striking. In Toulouse, for example, the twenty richest noble families doubled their income from land in the second half of the century **(48)**. The nobility, plus the wealthy merchant and legal families, owned 75 per cent of the wealth of Toulouse, although they constituted only a small fraction of the population. Yet a quarter of the townspeople were paupers **(49)**.

Similar inequalities existed in Orléans, whose population of 41-42,000 was dominated by a noble, clerical and rich commoner oligarchy of about 2,600. The 24,000 workers in Orléans ate inferior bread to their betters, wore clothing of cheaper and coarser materials, spent at least half their income on bread and were scourged by unemployment and mendicity in the 1780s **(47)**. In Paris the gap between the very rich minority, the wealthiest of whom were nobles possessing over 500,000 *livres,* and the impoverished mass of the people was still greater. The nobility, clergy, upper and middle bourgeoisie accounted for about 120,000 individuals, whilst the future *sans culottes* (artisans, small-shopkeepers and traders, wage-earners, clerks, journeymen and apprentices) numbered over 500,000 people. The capital also possessed a large floating population of at least 50,000 seething with large numbers of casual labourers, domestic servants, foot-loose immigrants, criminals and *gens sans aveu* **(74,** chs 2 and 3; **71,** ch. 2). There was, of course, nothing corresponding to the urban working class of post-industrial society. *Ouvrier* could mean an independent craftsman, a small workshop master, or even a substantial manufacturer, as well as an ordinary wage earner. The division between masters and men in small workshop industry was very blurred. Nevertheless, neither the French Revolution in general nor the Terror in particular can be understood without some grasp of the permanent underlying antagonism between rich and poor.

There was also increasing tension between the rich nobles at the apex of society and the wealthier commoners immediately beneath them. The traditional view that landed nobles were opposed by a rising bourgeoisie which had made money in trade and industry, and wished to make more by getting rid of 'feudalism' and furthering the growth of 'capitalism', has recently been convincingly challenged by Alfred Cobban and George V. Taylor **(29,** chs 5,14,15; **33-37)**. They point out that capitalists were thin on the ground and tended to stay clear of politics; between the nobility, itself subject to many variations of wealth and status, and the *haute bourgeoisie* or upper middle class, there was no sharp division of economic interest. Antagonism was social and ideological rather than economic. The social order of the *ancien régime* was based on aristocratic values: belief in the natural inequality of man, the traditional rights of birth, hereditary lands and offices, exemptions from sections of the law and the bulk of taxation. It appears that population increase and rising prices created wider social cleavages at all levels of society after 1770. Resentment among more prosperous commoners at the privileges and status of the nobility deepened, not least because the virtual noble monopoly of high posts in the Church, law, army and government did not diminish and might well have increased during the last years of the *ancien régime* (67; 98, ch. 2).

The impact of the ideas of the Enlightenment is difficult to assess in any precise way, but certainly affected considerable numbers of the nobility, the more educated commoners and some groups in lower social strata. Writers like Montesquieu, Diderot and d'Holbach argued that the principles of human society could be discovered, like those of the natural world, and then applied to the reformation of men and governments. Thus Europe was facing a new era of progress and improvement, which could bring about the perfectibility of man. Such optimism was an essential ingredient of the 'revolutionary spirit' after 1788. Belief in a new age of progress involved an assault on tradition; stress was laid, for example, on a new 'natural' hierarchy of property rather than on traditional birth and privilege. Even the Terror of 1793-94 was seen as partly an attempt to promote human improvement on a rational basis [doc. 24].

Although the Enlightenment was not primarily political, political inspiration was sought in the works of the *philosophes* by reforming monarchs, liberal nobles and the professional middle classes. The French *parlements*, in their struggle with the royal government in the 1760s and 1780s, invoked Montesquieu's belief in 'intermediary bodies' between ruler and people. They also pillaged the works of Rousseau, whose *Social Contract* (1762) developed the theory of the social contract, leading to the concepts of the 'sovereignty of the people' and the 'general will': the idea that society as a whole should decide its interests. Rousseau's emphasis on the freedom of the individual and on the equality of men as moral agents, had strong democratic implications (26, chs 1 and 2; 62, ch. 8). Conflict between monarch and *parlements* in the 1760s over royal administration and taxation resulted in the use by *parlements* of a good deal of potentially revolutionary language. Words like *citoyen, loi, patrie, constitution, nation, droit de la nation* and *cri de la nation* were stressed so much that they became revolutionary slogans in themselves (14, vol. i, ch. 14). The realization that the political ideas of the *philosophes* could be put into practice was deepened by the American Revolution, which seemed in European eyes a new enlightened process leading to a just society where men were free from the bankrupt European tradition. American federal and state constitutions were avidly studied and debated by the educated classes in France (15, part ii, ch. 3).

Yet the *parlements* were not the only source of disturbance during the reign of Louis XVI. Research by Professor Rudé has made us aware of a tradition of revolt on bread prices and wages that went back at least to the early 1770s (71; 72, chs 3-7). Arthur Young, the English agricultural expert and traveller in France in the late 1780s, wrote: 'The deficit would not have produced the Revolution but in concurrence with the price of bread.' Workers spent something like half their incomes on bread; the proportion could rise to 58 per cent in times of economic crisis and to a disastrous 88 per cent in the famine conditions of the midsummer of 1789 (73).

Despite government awareness that high bread prices meant food riots and popular disturbances, hence ministerial steps to ensure the provisioning of urban markets, riots still took place (74, ch. 3; 56). In 1774 there was the large-scale 'Flour war' (*guerre des farines*) in the Paris region, followed by food riots at Toulouse and Grenoble in 1778 and Rennes in 1785, as well as protests in 1785 and 1786 against the ring of customs posts recently erected around Paris. Strikes for higher wages and protests at the high price of basic consumer goods were also frequent. A wave of strikes in Lyon, the second city of France and the centre of the leading industrial region, led to the use of troops, bloodshed and executions. By 1789 over 18,000 workers in Lyon depended on public charity (57).

As yet, these popular movements were limited in their aims to bread-and-butter questions of wages, prices and working conditions; none of them involved any kind of coherent political criticism of the *ancien régime*. Such criticism was being developed by the liberal nobility and the professional middle classes from the ideas of the *philosophes* and disseminated through political discussion clubs, masonic lodges and learned societies until they formed links with the popular movement from 1788. The latter possessed considerable revolutionary potential. Distorted information, exaggerated rumours, songs, pictures and three-dimensional images could play on popular fears, especially of famine, and lead to a search for an individual, group or institutional scapegoat. This was to prove a constant factor in the Revolution, certainly until December 1794. If 'aristocrats' and the royal government could be substituted for the miller, baker and food-hoarder as 'enemies of the people', then the step from a food or wage riot to aggressive and violent revolutionary action was but a short one (75). In 1788 the aristocratic revolt began a movement which brought together middle-class and popular discontent with some common aims and common enemies. The result was the dramatic events of 1789.

THE ARISTOCRATIC REVOLT

The immediate cause of the French Revolution was the clash between the royal government and the aristocracy in 1787 and 1788. With a deficit of 112 million *livres* and government credit exhausted, France faced national bankruptcy. The four wars the country had waged between 1733 and 1783 had cost about 4,000 million *livres.* Drastic economies in government and court expenditure would save only 30 per cent of total expenses at the most. The problem for the government was how to find increasing revenue in an inflationary situation without attacking the fiscal privileges of the nobility and clergy, privileges which left them exempt from the bulk of taxation. This problem had no solution; indirect taxes on consumer goods proved insufficient and there would have to be increased revenue from direct taxation. In other words, the fiscal exemptions of the nobility, the clergy and the wealthier middle classes would have to be drastically modified.

Such reforms would make changes in the chaotic French administration so fundamental as to amount to a revolution. Not that there was really a possibility of carrying them through, for this needed more power than the French monarchy in fact possessed. Beneath the impressive surface of professional ministers, *intendants,* governors and military commanders lay bewildering disorder. Not only were the internal administrative units of the country confused and overlapping, but royal power was subject to major political checks from the powerfully organised Church, *parlements,* and provincial estates (**53**, ch. 1; 58; **61**; **42**, ch. 2). Poor communications, made no better by a mass of tolls and barriers, were a further hindrance to efficient administration from the centre.

Calonne, Controller-General of Finances since 1783, attempted in 1787 to come to grips with the financial crisis. An Assembly of Notables, hand picked for assumed docility, was presented with a programme of reform which included a new graduated land tax (**53**, ch. 1). However, Calonne's plans for fiscal reform were brusquely rejected and he was dismissed on 8 April. His successor, Brienne, could do no better, since his proposals for a modified land tax were also rejected. Before being dismissed on 25 May 1787 by Louis XVI, some leading Notables, especially Lafayette, argued that only 'a truly national assembly' could assent to drastic new taxation. Such a body, it was claimed, already existed in the form of the States-General *(Etats-généraux),* a gathering of the three traditional orders which had not met since 1614 (**53**, chs 1-3; **58**).

The first Assembly of the Notables marks the real beginning of the Revolution. The basic attitude of the majority of the aristocracy was now clearly revealed. Concern to maintain their fiscal privileges made them more hostile than ever to any strengthening of the royal government (**53**, ch. 5). The financial crisis, which had crippled the government since 1774 and had been aggravated by ruinous borrowing policies, was thrown into sharp relief. Moreover, it became apparent that financial reform was linked to administrative reform, which in turn depended on a considerable degree of fiscal equality. In short, the destruction of the *ancien régime* seemed inevitable. As Barnave pointed out, the Crown must either become a military despotism and destroy ancient institutions and privileges by force, or it must transform itself into some sort of constitutional monarchy. The tragedy of Louis XVI and his ministers was that neither alternative was really practicable (**74**, ch. 5; **41**, ch. 4; **17**, ch. 2).

Some attempt was made at a policy of force, which immediately led to what Mathiez called 'the noble revolt'. In July 1787 Brienne tried and failed to persuade the *parlement* of Paris to accept the reforms rejected by the Notables. The *parlements*, law courts composed of noble magistrates rather than 'parliaments' with legislative powers, again put forward their longstanding claim to register royal decrees and to protest at government legislation, claims which aimed at thwarting 'absolute monarchy' and which had involved them in head-on clashes with the royal government in the 1760s and 1770s (**61**). In challenging royal ministers by scuttling financial reform, the *parlements* posed as the defenders of popular 'rights' and 'liberties'. When the Paris *parlement* rejected Brienne's reforms as 'contrary to the rights of the nation'. it was exiled to Troyes, while its obstinacy was endorsed by most of the other *parlements* and by street demonstrations of law clerks and youths in Paris (**53**, chs 4-6).

Brienne, evading reiterated demands for the calling of the States-General, recalled the *parlement* of Paris in September 1787 amid anti-government riots; these were followed by further demonstrations when middle-class citizens and members of the legal profession were joined by journeymen and workers living near the *palais de Justice*. Thus the *menu peuple* of Paris were drawn into political rioting for the first time (**71**, ch. 3; **59**). Tracts and pamphlets persuaded them that the aristocratic *parlements* were defending popular rights against 'despotism' (**60**). Furthermore, the weaknesses of the forces of order in Paris were clearly revealed, something the crowd was to remember in April and July 1789 (**74**, ch. 4).

When the *parlement* still refused to accept new taxes and on 19 November reiterated its demand for the calling of the States-General a renewed battle between the *parlement* and the monarchy began and lasted six months, deepening the financial crisis, robbing the government of its reforming zeal and spreading defiance of the government both to the nobility in general and to the middle classes (**74**, ch. 5). Louis XVI saw clearly enough that the *parlements*, although posing as the champion of the 'rights of the nation', sought to obtain rule by the aristocracy alone. Again the government resorted to force. Leading *parlementaires* were arrested in May 1788 and the *parlements* themselves deprived of many of their powers. The result was an outburst of disorder in various parts of the country, when opposition to the government was stiffened by the effects of unemployment and high commodity prices after the bad harvest of 1788. Royal judges and officials were mobbed in Paris and Toulouse; the aristocracy in Franche-Comté demanded restoration of the provincial estates; there were riots against the *intendant* in Brittany and a popular rising against royal troops in Dauphiné. In Grenoble, the liberal aristocracy and the middle classes came together to demand the end of fiscal privileges and the entry of commoners to all offices (**54**).

Faced by the united opposition of the judicial, clerical and lay aristocracy, as well as by a breakdown of royal authority in the provinces, the government was obliged to surrender. Brienne was succeeded by Necker, and on 8 August it was agreed that the States-General should meet at Versailles on 1 May 1789. Although there were street demonstrations when the king reinstated the *parlements* on 23 September, popular enthusiasm for the latter did not last long. For the Paris *parlement* declared that the States-General should be convoked according to the forms of 1614: that is, an equal number of representatives for each order and the three orders voting separately. Thus the clergy and the nobility would be able to impose their will on the third estate of commoners and retain their privileges. In June a new 'patriot party' had begun to take shape, composed of *philosophes*, lawyers, magistrates, journalists and liberal nobles. After September it was no longer willing to support the *parlements* in their struggle against the middle classes, for the *parlementaires* seemed to ignore the social ambitions of the middle class and the desire of many 'patriots' to see the end of privilege and 'feudalism'. During the autumn and winter of 1788 there took place a realignment of revolutionary forces. What had been a clash between the monarchy and the aristocracy, the latter being generally supported by many groups of commoners, now became a broad conflict between the privileged and the unprivileged. The monarchial and aristocratic antagonists of 1787-88 were to be pushed together in 1789 to face the challenge of the third estate. On close inspection, matters were not quite so clearcut, for the commoners found allies among the liberal nobles, sections of the higher and lower clergy and some progressive magistrates.

Before the end of 1788 the patriot party, organised in clubs, societies and corresponding committees, was making the running by putting forward the key ideas which were to dominate the thinking of the third estate in the spring and summer of 1789: the desirability of a declaration of rights, the idea of 'national sovereignty' and the need for a constitution. Over 2,500 pamphlets were circulated in late 1788 and early 1789. Such steps involved a direct collision with the traditional, hierarchical, privileged structure of French society. The immediate issue, however, was the convocation of the States-General. How many deputies should be elected for each order? How would they vote? Partly because of pressure of public opinion and partly to punish the nobility for their opposition to the royal government, the king and Necker accepted the principle of double representation for the third estate. The question of voting by head or by order was shelved until the actual meeting of the States-General **(20,** part i, ch. 1; **17,** ch. 3).

The events of 1789 must be considered against a background of intense economic crisis, a result of the catastrophic harvest of 1788, which had been preceded by drought and storms. Bread prices increased to starvation levels and created widespread unrest, resulting in attacks on granaries, popular price fixing of bread *(taxation populaire)* and rioting against bakers, farmers, corn dealers, game laws and royal taxes. Ancillary causes of distress and disturbance were the decline of the wine trade and the flood of cheap English manufactures into France **(73; 74,** ch. 6; **75; 52,** ch. **6).** The common people tended to blame the government rather than the weather or English industrial enterprise. Unemployed workers blamed it for concluding the Eden treaty with England in 1786, or suspected it of being in league with grain hoarders and speculators - the *pacte de famine.*

Widespread hunger also led to exceptionally violent opposition to government taxation, especially the indirect taxes on food and drink, and to the tolls and duties levied on most food products. In such circumstances, the tax exemptions of so many of the rich were bitterly resented. The grievances of wage-earners, craftsmen, wine-producers and small traders were allied to those of the mass of the peasants against tithes, seigneurial dues and hunting rights. Hence a vast popular movement appeared during the winter of 1788-89, when the economic and political crises became welded together and when the patriot party and the *menu peuple* joined forces against the government, the aristocracy, and the social and political system of the *ancien régime.*

4   Liberal Revolution 1789-92

QUATRE-VINGT-NEUF

Compared with the disorder in the capital and the provinces during the early months of 1789, the meeting of the States-General at Versailles and the conflict which followed seemed a very gentlemanly affair. Although the king and the aristocracy still intended to govern the nation, their will to do so was soon shaken by the confidence of the third estate, who felt that a new age was approaching and the *ancien régime* on its last legs. As Sieyès put it in his famous pamphlet *Qu'est ce que le Tiers État?* in January 1789: 'What is the third estate? Everything. What has it been until the present time? Nothing. What does it ask? To become something.' The 561 deputies for the first two orders did not present a united front to defend privilege. Among the nobles there were about ninety who had been connected with the 'patriot party' and were willing to go a considerable way in the direction of liberty and equality. Moreover, the provincial nobility, the most anxious to defend hierarchy and privilege, had no love for the court nobility, whom they saw as monopolising the highest posts and adopting airs of superiority. Neither did they much care for those nobles who had been influenced by the *philosophes*.

Divisions were also apparent within the first estate, where the lower clergy were in conflict with the bishops and religious orders over plural livings and the low stipend of the ordinary *curé*. Hence of the 291 clerical deputies, there were about 200 *curés* who were to prove willing to join the third estate in its struggle against the king and his ministers. It is true that there were also divisions among the third estate, for example on the question of the abolition of feudal rights, on free trade and on the suppression of corporations, but these remained largely beneath the surface until August. The 578 deputies of the third estate included about 400 lawyers and officials in the royal administration and about a hundred bankers, merchants and industrialists, although few of the latter operated on a large scale. There were also a number of 'intellectuals' — scientists, economists and writers — as well as some prominent refugees from the privileged orders such as Sieyès and Mirabeau. Certainly the third estate did not lack

28

confidence. Its leaders exuded what might be termed the 'revolutionary spirit': a mixture of optimism, idealism, hope and excitement. They believed that their work was for the good of humanity in general, as well as for that of the French people (52, ch. 3)

Although procedural wrangling lasted over a month, the third estate was sustained by the lists of grievances *(cahiers)* of the commoners and by the expanding newspaper press, as well as by the fact that the royal government had prepared no detailed policies (74, ch. 7). Hence the commons, as they began to call themselves, held firm against the king and the intransigent majority of the nobility; on 17 June it declared itself the 'National Assembly' and on 20 June swore the Tennis Court Oath, to remain in session until a constitution had been established. Within a few days a majority of clerical deputies and a number of nobles joined the National Assembly. A royal session of 23 June proved to be the swansong of the *ancien régime,* for the king's reforming programme made little impression and he was obliged to give way. Not only were his ministers divided, but he lacked a sufficient concentration of troops at Versailles to dissolve the National Assembly in the face of public opinion, particularly the Paris crowd. Knowledge that the people were hungry, suspicious of the government and ready to challenge the throne, did a good deal to sap the morale of the monarchy and boost that of the National Assembly (22, book ii, ch. 2; 52, ch. 5)

The *ancien régime* was brought down by both the third estate at Versailles and by the people of Paris and the provinces. After the meeting of the States-General the economic crisis had deepened. The stormy, wet spring meant that the 1789 harvest would be late. Imports of grain proved insufficient to prevent rapid price increases; indeed it was on 14 July that the price of grain and bread in Paris reached the highest since 1715. Prices were forcibly reduced by the urban crowds; peasants in a number of areas refused to pay tithes; the forces of order seemed powerless to resist and the law appeared to be petrified (74, ch. 7).

Popular disturbances in the spring of 1789 also owed something to exasperation with the stalemate at Versailles. The importance of fear and rumour in the popular movement was first analysed and emphasised by Lefebvre in *La Grande Peur de 1789* (1932). Both the people and the deputies of the third estate believed that the king would try to disperse the States-General. There was also almost universal belief in the 'aristocratic plot', for plots tended to explain almost everything to the popular mind throughout the Revolution. The nobility, it was rumoured, were plotting to overthrow the third estate and to seize power; it was 'plotters' who were in league with grain speculators and hoarders in a 'famine pact' to starve the people into submission. Increasing numbers of brigands, a consequence of poverty and unemployment, were feared to be the shock troops of the plotters, ready to lay waste the country-side at the appropriate signal [doc. 16]. Thus the high price of bread, the stagnation of the States-General for a long period and the spread of brigandage became connected in the popular mind as key ingredients in a plot to subdue the people. Many of the hundreds of 'loyal addresses' sent to Versailles warned the deputies to be on their guard against a sudden show of force by the king and the nobility (52, ch. 6; 74, ch. 7). As a consequence of fear and rumour, the people began to arm, forming local militia or 'peasant guards' for defence against 'brigands'. By early July, a substantial area of France was under arms, ready to stand by the third estate if the king attempted to dissolve the National Assembly. In reality, as Jacques Godechot has pointed out, the forces available to the king were much less numerous and reliable than popular imagination credited. Troops were sapped by revolutionary propaganda and exhausted by constant activity against rioters. Fragmentation of units into small detachments to deal with scattered disturbances seriously weakened the chain of command. Many soldiers shared the antagonism of the people towards the privileged orders; non-commis-sioned officers resented their exclusion from the officer corps in many branches of the army. In late June the crack *gardes-françaises* began fraternising with the crowd; even some of the Swiss guards proved disloyal. If the king were persuaded to attempt a show of force in a desperate last-minute attempt to save the *ancien régime,* then a dispersed, disorganised and unreliable army would be faced by an armed and enthusiastic people who were in an almost permanent state of insurrection (74, ch. 7; 59; 78)

Such an attempt was made from 22 June onwards, when the king gave marching orders summoning troops to Paris. By 4 July there were 30,000 soldiers in Paris and the surrounding area and the king refused requests from an alarmed National Assembly that he remove them. The inevitable clash came when the king dismissed the 'liberal' Necker on 11 July without having clear plans on what to do next. Such indecision allowed the pamphleteers and journalists under the aegis of the Duc d'Orléans at the Palais Royal, the 407 electors of the Paris third estate at the Hôtel de Ville and the *menu peuple* of Paris to take the initiative (74, ch. 8). News of Necker's dismissal prompted the risings which led to the fall of the Bastille and the collapse of the *ancien régime,* risings which aimed at forestalling the rumoured dissolu-tion of the National Assembly and an armed *coup* against the capital.

On Sunday 12 July crowds closed the Paris theatres, clashed with dragoons and occupied the Tuileries palace. Throughout the night of 12-13 July the tocsin rang and sections of the crowd searched the city for arms. Attention was then turned to the fifty-four customs posts *(barrières)*, built in 1785 to levy duty on goods entering the capital. Forty of these were set on fire and the ten-foot wall demolished in places; prisons were attacked, especially those suspected of hoarding grain or arms. Order in Paris had almost completely broken down, whilst news of Necker's departure roused passions throughout France, where banks were attacked, arms seized and troops harassed.

A climax was reached with the massive *journée* of 14 July, the day of the taking of the Bastille. The crowd, fearful of the government counter-attack, set off to capture 30,000 muskets from the *Invalides* and 250 barrels of gunpowder, plus cartridges, from the Bastille, an old fortress used as a prison. A crowd of 8,000 overwhelmed the *Invalides*, grabbed the muskets and four cannon, and then marched on the Bastille, which, apart from being also an arms depot, stood as a symbol of royal 'despotism' whose guns menaced the populous Faubourg Saint-Antoine. The governor could not be persuaded to withdraw his cannon or hand over the arms; so the Bastille was attacked and taken, largely by the efforts of a hundred *gardes-françaises* who had defected to the people. Several of the defenders were massacred; of the attackers, ninety-eight were killed and seventy-three injured.

Royalist and conservative historians later claimed that the *vainqueurs de la Bastille* were *canaille* and criminals in the pay of freemasons, Orléanists and *philosophes.* Yet five-sixths of the 700 to 800 whose occupations and addresses are known were artisans, masters or journey-men, such as joiners, locksmiths, cobblers, shopkeepers and clockmakers. The remaining sixth included more prosperous tradesmen, soldiers and officers, and members of the professions. All lived within two kilometres of the Bastille, though at least half were newly arrived from the provinces. The footloose, the vagabonds, the criminals and the very poor do not appear to have been involved. It is important to remember that the crowd had little to beat; large numbers of troops were unreliable; so were the 1,500 Paris police, disillusioned by lack of government support. Rumours of a march on Paris by determined troops lacked substance; so did fears of an aristocratic plot **(74**, ch. 9; **78)**.

Although the king's diary entry for 14 July was *'Rien',* the immediate consequences of the popular victory were soon visible. Royal plans for a counteroffensive against Paris and a royal session at Versailles to overawe the third estate had to be abandoned. After meeting his advisers. Louis agreed to recall Necker and order the withdrawal of troops from Paris and Versailles. Three days after the fall of the

Bastille, he was persuaded to go to Paris with a procession of deputies, to speak briefly from the steps of the Hôtel de Ville and to put in his hat the new revolutionary cockade of red, white and blue. Thomas Jefferson, American ambassador in Paris commented: 'Such an *amende honorable* . . . no sovereign ever made, and no people ever received.' News of the fall of the Bastille was reported all over the world, usually in terms of the dawning of a new age of liberty; there was dancing even in the streets of St Petersburg. In France itself there was widespread rejoicing. The first issue of the newspaper *Les Révolutions de Paris* on 17 July declared: 'The events of that glorious day will astonish our enemies, and foretell at last the triumph of justice and liberty.' The events of 12-17 July marked the end of royal absolutism and the transfer of sovereign authority to the National Assembly, now recognised by the king. The court party began to disintegrate and some prominent court nobles left for the frontier. Censorship of the press disappeared. In Paris there was a revolution in municipal government: power passed into the hands of the committee of property-owning electors who formed the new Paris Commune and the National Guard. Some tension existed not far below the surface, for the electors were anxious about the possible destruction of property and the threat of 'anarchy'; they were therefore reluctant to allow the indiscriminate distribution of arms. Neither did they welcome the attacks on the *barrières* and the prisons; in fact the customs posts were quickly restored. Such tensions and anxieties were to reappear in the future, but in July 1789 they were swept aside by popular enthusiasm for liberty and by fears of an aristocratic plot.

THE DOWNFALL OF THE *ANCIEN RÉGIME*

It is possible to view the events of July as the climax of a national revolution which had its origins in the *révolte nobilaire* and began in earnest in January 1789. The same was true of the creation of citizen militias. If the people of the capital were stimulated by the example of the provinces, which so many of them had only recently left, the process was reversed after the fall of the Bastille. Provincial revolutionaries were now inspired by events in Paris. Municipal revolutions took place; some were unsuccessful, but many others succeeded in removing established oligarchies, controlling the price of bread, and creating companies of the National Guard, designed, as in Paris, to curb both aristocratic reaction and popular disturbances (82). As *intendants* fled, the breakdown of royal authority and the *de facto* decentralisation of French local government were both confirmed.

News of the fall of the Bastille also provided further incitement for the peasant revolt. The failure of the National Assembly to tackle the question of peasant grievances was put down to machinations of the 'aristocratic plot'. Feudal dues weighed more heavily on the peasants in a time of famine, when bread prices were even higher than in Paris and the large towns. Landlords were widely suspected of food hoarding. Since the spring, there had been increasing peasant attacks on the walls and fences of enclosed fields, accompanied by reoccupation of former common lands and suspension of the payment of tithes and feudal dues. From 20 July to 6 August the 'Great Fear' was at its height. Rumours of an aristocratic counter-revolution, where *émigrés* after 14 July would return at the head of hordes of Piedmontese or Spanish brigands and foreign mercenaries, were fed by the dispersal of military units from Paris to the countryside and by the despatch of companies from the towns to requisition grain. Great alarm spread over most of France; the 'brigands', it was alleged, would burn the ripening corn in the fields as the crucial step in the *pacte de famine*. When the brigands failed to materialise, the peasants turned on the *châteaux*, many of which were razed to the ground when the manorial rolls, recording seignorial obligations, had been destroyed (**52**, ch. 10; **81**; **98**, ch. 4) [**doc. 2**]

Although peasant violence had been endemic since the beginning of the year, the revolt of late July and early August took the National Assembly very much unawares. With its victory over the king and the court consummated on the 14 July, the Assembly hoped to get on with its self-appointed task of preparing a Declaration of Rights and a Constitution. It had never fully approved of the violence in Paris and the municipalities, but at least such violence had been largely inspired by middle-class leaders who usually showed an appropriate respect for private property. But the peasant revolt had been carried through by a rural proletariat which had attacked property indiscriminately, whether it was that of the *seigneurs* or not. Moreover, peasants were against economic freedom, preferring, on the contrary, regulation of the grain trade and bread prices and restoration of traditional agrarian organisation. These were some of the key demands of the rural *cahiers,* which many members of the Assembly had had a hand in erasing before setting off for Versailles. Members of the third estate had never intended to attack seigneurial rights; indeed some of them were owners of such rights. Besides, if feudal property were to be destroyed, then it should be done by legal methods with due compensation, not by unbridled insurrection (**52**, ch. 11; **18**, ch. 3).

Despite these misgivings about the peasant rebellion, the Assembly was forced to make concessions. Public order and private property could be maintained only by giving legal sanction to the peasants' action or by a full-scale repression of the peasantry. Dispersal of military forces made the second alternative impracticable. In any case, the Assembly needed the support of the peasants. On the night of 4 August, wealthy members of the liberal aristocracy took the lead in renouncing their feudal privileges. Impassioned speeches built up into a crescendo of renunciation. Seignorial justice, hunting rights, fiscal exemptions, tithes in kind, venal judicial offices: all were abandoned. Provincial, corporate and municipal privileges were also renounced. When emotion evaporated somewhat during the next few days, the conservative instincts of many property-owners and lawyers in the Assembly reasserted themselves. It turned out that the 'feudal *régime*' was not, as had been announced 'entirely destroyed'; contractual feudal dues were to be subject to redemption by individual purchase, a qualification which disillusioned the peasants. As things turned out, it did not much matter; for peasants dug in their heels and refused to pay anything. A decree of the Convention in July 1793 cancelled the remaining debt (18, ch. 3; 33, ch. 5).

The Declaration of Rights of 26 August 1789 was an attempt not only to outshine the English Bill of Rights and the American Declaration of Independence, but also to take the wind out of the sails of counter-revolution and guide the Assembly in its subsequent task of drawing up a constitution. Middle-class individualism provided the essential spirit of the Declaration [doc. 3]. The two fundamental doctrines stated were natural rights and national sovereignty. 'Liberty, property, security and resistance to oppression' were the natural rights, leading on to equality in taxation and before the law. Freedom of speech, liberty of the press and (rather obliquely) toleration of religious opinion were also granted. All citizens had the right to share in making the laws, either personally or through representatives.

The middle-class spirit of the document very much came out in the emphasis on property as 'an inviolable and sacred right' and on the necessity for compensation if property (that is, feudal dues) were expropriated. Political and social equality were, significantly, not mentioned. Neither were rights of petition and assembly, education or poor relief. Despite these restrictions, there remains some justification for Aulard's description of the Declaration as 'the death certificate of the *ancien régime*'. for much of it looked to the past. The sovereignty of the people meant that France was no longer the personal property of the monarch. That no man could be arrested or detained other than under the law put an end to arbitrary arrest. Presumed innocence meant no restoration of torture. Resistance to oppression gave legal sanction to the insurrection of 14 July. Thus the document was more a product of specific historical circumstances than an abstract appeal to posterity. It expressed satisfaction with the destruction of the *ancien régime* and the confidence of the energetic leaders of the Assembly who felt that they were, in the words of Lefebvre, 'on their way to transforming the world' (**52**, ch. 12).

Not until October, however, were the gains of the summer of 1789 consolidated. The king refused to accept either the decrees of August on feudal rights or the Declaration of Rights, and still possessed the loyalty of the rump of a counter-revolutionary court party. There was also a group of social conservatives, the *monarchiens,* in the Assembly, who aimed at providing France with a constitutional monarchy in which the king would have the power of veto and the nobility an upper chamber to restrain the activities of the Assembly. Only substantial property owners would possess the franchise. In the event, the suggestion for an upper chamber was rejected, but the question of the veto caused such prolonged debate and political manoeuvring that the progress of the Revolution seemed almost at a halt (**83**). Yet a further breakthrough began in mid-September when the king, under increasing pressure from the Assembly to endorse the August decrees, summoned the Flanders regiment to Versailles. They were welcomed at a banquet where the revolutionary cockade was trampled underfoot in an orgy of royalist fervour. News of this in Paris acted as a goad to the people, who, prompted by radical journalists, demanded that the king be removed from Versailles and the 'corrupt' influence of the court. Despite the good harvest of 1789, the price of bread had risen again, for drought had put many corn mills out of action [**doc.4**]. On 5 October market women set off to march to Versailles, reinforced by 20,000 of the Paris National Guard, led by Lafayette. At Versailles they persuaded the king and the royal family to leave for Paris, soon to be followed by the National Assembly. Before departing, the king accepted the August decrees and the Declaration of Rights.

Thus the people of Paris had again intervened at a decisive moment and secured the consolidation of the gains of the Revolution of the summer. Discredited by the 'march to Versailles'. the *monarchien* party, headed by Mounier, collapsed, a number of members fleeing abroad. All this had taken place because, as in July, the middle-class members of the Assembly had been willing to work in partnership with the Paris *menu peuple.* Once more, this marriage of convenience had been forced by royal intransigence. There could no longer be any compromise between the Court and the Revolution. The alliance between Assembly and people remained something of an uneasy one, for insurrection was something which could all too easily be turned against the educated and propertied classes. Hence the Assembly declared martial law, censored the extremist press and imposed the death penalty for sedition. Once the Assembly's victory over monarch and aristocracy had been secured, it sought a period of social and political stability during which a constitution could be drawn up and French institutions reconstructed on Revolutionary principles (71, ch. 5; 18 ch. 4; 52, ch. 15; 98, ch. 4).

The Revolution of 1789 was over and the *ancien régime* was beyond revival. Absolute monarchy had fallen and would be succeeded by a constitution based on equality before the law. It is as well to keep in mind that the Revolution of 1789 was baptised in violence and that violence ran through the Revolution; the September Massacres of 1792, the great Terror of 1793-94 and the blood bath of Thermidor were only peaks in a violent revolutionary landscape. The *ancien régime* in 1789 was, as Lefebvre emphasised, destroyed by force rather than by speechifying at Versailles (52, conclusion). The obstinacy of the monarchy and the intransigence of most of the nobility made a peaceful evolution, desired as no doubt it was by many lawyers in the Assembly, impossible.

RECONSTRUCTION

The good harvest of 1789 meant that 1790 was a relatively calm year as far as violence and disorder were concerned. What conflicts there were tended to be sporadic and localised. So the Constituent Assembly was able to get on with its task of constitution-making. France was to be a constitutional monarchy, but the power of the king and his ministers was to be severely restricted. While the monarch could appoint ministers, they were to be responsible to the legislature and a decision to go to war had to be confirmed by the Assembly. The latter had full control of financial legislation and the king was given only a four-year 'suspensive veto' over other legislation. Chances of a royalist *coup* were weakened by loosening the control of the king over the army and strengthening the National Guard under the aegis of local authorities. Power was to rest largely in the hands of the Constituent Assembly; total legislative power was augmented by much more executive power than was enjoyed by the legislatures of England and the United States.

In spite of article 14 of the Declaration of Rights, the suffrage was restricted, the right to vote being confined to 'active' citizens: those over twenty-five with residential qualifications and paying taxes to the equivalent value of three days unskilled labour. However, the system of indirect election of the third estate in 1789 was retained. Primary voters elected secondary assemblies, members of which had to pay taxes equivalent to ten days labour. Secondary assemblies chose the deputies, who were required to pay a silver mark (*52 livres*) in taxes. As Sieyés argued, at each level a certain amount of wealth guaranteed some measure of economic independence, education and leisure time, held to be essential for political participation. Just how narrow the franchise was in practice is not easily ascertained, for there were considerable regional variations, mainly because of the different values attached to three days unskilled labour. Professor Palmer calculates that almost 70 men in every 100, that is, the heads of most households, could vote in primary elections; 50 in 100 in secondary elections; and 1 in 100 was able to stand as deputy (14, vol. i, appendix 5). Almost a quarter of adult males were 'passive' citizens, excluded from voting. Nevertheless, this franchise was the most liberal in Europe at the time and more democratic than historians like Louis Blanc, Aulard and Mathiez believed.

Constitution-making was paralleled by administrative, judicial, financial and ecclesiastical reform. Nobility and titles were abolished; so were the old offices, though not without compensation for the owners. Hence the principle of the 'career open to talents' was furthered. A new three-tier uniform system of local government was introduced, whereby departments, districts and communes replaced the jumbled medieval administrative map of the *ancien régime.* At each level, both councils and local government officials were elected by active citizens. To some extent the new structure marked the confirmation of a system that had already come into being and therefore represented collaboration with the inevitable; for the municipal revolts of the summer of 1789 had effectively decentralised government. The loss of royal authority could not be regained by the Assembly in Paris, at least not in conditions of peacetime. France therefore became, in effect, a loose federation of departments and districts, with minimal control from the capital. In Paris itself the commune was to become the rival of the national legislature in 1792.

The complex, arbitrary and expensive judicial system of the *ancien régime* was also swept away. In line with the Declaration of Rights, justice was to be free and men equal before the law. New courts and tribunals were established at each level of local government, with a central court of appeal and, a rather sinister touch, a high court for cases of treason. Judges and magistrates were elected from a panel of qualified candidates; criminal cases were to be tried by jury. At a time when much of the latent savagery of the revolutionary situation had not yet broken the surface, some of the humane ideals of the Enlightenment could be put into practice: torture, branding and hanging were abolished. Capital punishment, retained after prolonged and intense debate, was to be by decapitation, a fate hitherto reserved for the nobility.

Financial stability was the most difficult problem facing the Assembly and one which it conspicuously failed to solve. Too many people, including a high proportion of peasants, imagined that taxation of any real weight had gone for good with the disappearance of privilege and exemption. New taxes on land, property and income made little impression on the deficit, especially when many refused to pay. Of the numerous schemes considered to evade national bankruptcy, the most important was the decision in November 1789 to appropriate and nationalise the estates of the Church and put them up for sale. In return, the state would assume the responsibilities of the Church for education and poor relief, as well as paying clerical salaries. Until the lands could be sold, *assignats* were issued. Originally interest-bearing government bonds. convertible into Church lands, the *assignats* soon became transformed into inconvertible paper currency. No doubt their introduction avoided imminent bankruptcy, but at the price of subsequent inflation, which promoted economic disorder and social unrest. The financial problem was, therefore, not so much solved as postponed.

There was rather more to the sale of Church lands than the question of finance. Many members of the Assembly saw it as a strategic move against an aristocratic reaction. Not only would a salaried clergy be dependent on the revolutionary *régime,* but the sale would also create a new class of proprietors whose interests were bound up with the Revolution and who would therefore be prepared to defend it against counter-revolution both inside and outside France. Certainly there were many municipalities and families, including aristocratic families, who had cast envious eyes on lucrative Church property. In the great 'national auction', prices were relatively low and payment could be made in instalments, especially advantageous in inflationary conditions. Comparatively little of the Church land was sold in small lots; most went to those with capital: the middle classes and richer peasants. The sale was not intended to be the instrument of serious social and economic levelling **(94)**. Henceforth there were hard material interests at the core of the Revolution. Whatever the nature of the *régime,* from Thermidor to Napoleon to the Restoration, nobody seriously planned to restore the pattern of landed proprietorship of pre-1789. In 1801 the Pope accepted that Church lands had gone for ever. As it was, however, the sale of Church lands united the rising, active groups in French society against the crowned heads of Europe, while at the same time embittering relations between town and country, for anticlericalism flourished in the towns rather than the countryside. At the head of the Revolution, for the moment, were a 'new bourgeoisie of landowners', to borrow Cobban's phrase, who knew that any future reaction could go only so far **(33,** ch. 8; **18,** ch. 5; **85,** ch. 4; **98,** ch. 5).

None of these reforms went against the grain of the remarkable spirit of national unity that had existed since the summer of 1789. Nor did the early ecclesiastical reforms of the National Assembly. The Church had suffered from a deep fissure between its privileged and unprivileged members; wealth and property were concentrated in the hands of noble prelates at the top of the ecclesiastical hierarchy. The status, privileges and right of self-taxation possessed by the Church conflicted with fundamental Revolutionary principles. Moreover, the bulk of the clerical *cahiers* had demanded reform of the most flagrant abuses and three hundred clerical deputies were prepared to help the Assembly in what they regarded as the purification and regeneration of the Church. Nor were the lay deputies the anticlericals, unbelievers, *philosophes,* Protestants and Jansenists of legend. 'In the great majority', wrote Mathiez, 'they were sincere Catholics', although, of course, in the Gallican tradition. There was as yet no widespread desire to destroy the Church or to deny its mission to the people. Although the Church lost its corporate status, right of self-taxation and independent administration on 4 August 1789, it was to remain the official Church of France. Religious toleration in the Declaration of Rights was as grudging as it was oblique. What is more, payment by the state would make a great many clergy better off in material terms. So not even the nationalisation of Church lands or the abolition of the contemplative orders roused the opposition of the clergy.

Yet conflict lay not far beneath the surface. At bottom there was a dilemma: how could an established state religion, with acknowledged influence over men's minds and hearts, be compatible with the revolutionary doctrines of liberty and equality? Such a conflict of principle might have been avoided by a careful skirting of the basic issues. Unfortunately the Assembly was in no mood for *finesse.* Not only was it under pressure from the vociferous and anticlerical people of Paris, but the submissiveness of the clergy in 1789 and 1790 promoted overconfidence and a belief that both Church and Pope would accept almost anything. As yet, however, the Assembly's reforms were, in the eyes of the Church, a more or less legitimate exercise of temporal power. To touch on the spiritual authority of the Church was an entirely different matter. Such an intrusion came with the oath of 27 November 1790 which followed the Civil Constitution of the clergy. This marked a crucial point in the Revolution, for it meant the end of the period of national unity and the real beginning of civil war and counter-revolution. Aristocrats and *émigrés* were henceforward to enjoy a substantial measure of popular support in France.

Religious schism resulted not so much from what was done, as from the way in which it was done. Everyone agreed that, tithes having been abolished and Church lands sold, legislation was necessary to put the Church on a different footing. The Civil Constitution of the Clergy, agreed on 12 July 1790, was in many ways a sensible settlement. Chapters were abolished, dioceses reduced in number, parishes reorganised according to a more logical pattern, the aristocratic monopoly of high Church office eliminated and reasonable salaries guaranteed to priests. Bishops and priests were to be elected by active citizens – a more contentious reform. In addition, some clerics stood to lose from the suppression of many parishes. Even so, the clergy did not rush to repudiate the Civil Constitution. They demanded that the proposals be submitted to a synod of the whole Church: *il faut consulter l'Église.* To the Assembly, a synod seemed an unacceptable challenge to the principle of national sovereignty and a platform for reactionaries; the Church ought not to pretend to dictate to the state. The dispute now became one about authority: 'the mood of the day was proud, suspicious, fearful, Gallican, erastian, anti-clerical' (85, ch. 5). Tension mounted throughout the country as the Pope delayed comment. But the Assembly was in no mood for delay, whilst local authorities and clubs began to take matters into their own hands. Not doubting that Pope Pius VI would eventually yield, the Assembly brought matters rapidly – too rapidly – to a head by demanding that all clergy take an oath of loyalty to the nation, the law, the king and the constitution [doc. 5].

To the surprise and anger of the Assembly, only a third of its clerical members agreed to take the oath, despite the presence of a noisy anti-clerical crowd outside the hall. In the country as a whole only seven bishops out of 160 accepted, and three of them were unbelievers. The clergy split about half and half, with considerable regional and local variations. Deep animosities were spread across the country; France was geographically split, for traditionally devout areas like the west, north and north-east rejected the 'constitutional' Church, whilst the centre, the Ile de France and the south-east largely accepted it. Many sincere men had to decide according to their conscience, or were put under pressure by theologians, their families, or the locality they served. It was often difficult to make a considered decision when 'constitutional' priests could be stoned and chased out of 'non-juring' areas, and 'refractory' priests could be met with cries of *'le serment ou la lanterne!'* Such a cruel tragedy could have been avoided by more patience and skill on the side of the Assembly. The nation was fissured, whatever the Revolutionary leaders might say; families and friends were divided. As Professor Hampson has pointed out: 'the anticlerical issue split the nation along different lines from its political and economic divisions' (18, ch. 4).

Many peasants were turned against the Revolution for the first time; the *émigrés* suddenly acquired a conscience. Those who had defied the Assembly were logically drawn towards the camp fires of counter-revolution. 'Patriot' became a term for those attending the 'constitutional' mass, and 'aristocrat' for those who did not (93, ch. 11). Many were pushed, both by hostile crowds and by municipalities given extra-legal powers to bully the non-jurors. The theoretical toleration granted by the Declaration of Rights proved to be worth very little. Indeed, the increasing hostility of the Revolution towards the non-juring clergy began to rub off on the constitutional clergy and lay the ground for the dechristianisation campaign in late 1783. It was to be years before the fact that France was still essentially a Catholic country became fully apparent and before Frenchmen realised that what many of them wanted was not endorsed by their womenfolk. Meanwhile, the gaping breach over the Church augured badly for the operation of a constitution which demanded a good deal of national unity and goodwill on all sides (40, ch. 2).

PART THREE

Jacobins and Sans Culottes

5 The Fall of the Monarchy

10 AUGUST 1792

On the morning of 10 August 1792 an insurrectionary force of about 20,000 attacked the Tuileries, although the king and his family had already fled the palace and taken refuge in the nearby Assembly. The besiegers consisted of Parisian *sans culottes,* National Guards who had deserted the royal cause and *fédérés* from Marseilles, Brest, Rouen and other towns. Because the bulk of the National Guard from the prosperous western districts of the capital had become alienated from the constitutional monarchy and absented themselves from the struggle, only the Swiss guards and gentlemen-grenadiers resisted. They were quickly and savagely overcome. About 600 Swiss were massacred, whilst about 300 *sans culottes* and 90 *fédérés* were killed or wounded. Far from being the 'bandits' and 'brigands' of counter-revolutionary legend, most of the *sectionnaires* involved were petty tradesmen and craftsmen from the Paris *faubourgs* [doc.7].

The consequences of the 10 August were momentous. In his newspaper *Le Défenseur de la Constitution,* Robespiere claimed that a new France would now be able to rule its destinies because of 'the most gorgeous revolution which has ever honoured humanity. . . that of equality, justice and reason'. Historians have seen it as a 'second revolution', which shifted the Revolution of 1789 in a new, radical direction. Marcel Reinhard, for example, regards the second assault on the Tuileries as 'the bloody dawn of a second revolution, the creation of a Jacobin republic, of a war government, of what some hoped would be political democracy and others social democracy' (**96**, ch. 21). Albert Soboul writes that 'this second revolution integrated the people into the nation and marked the advent of political democracy' (**20**, part i, ch. 5). On the evening of 10 August the king was suspended from office and France became a Republic in the following month. Royal guards were massacred or imprisoned, while the liberal nobles who had committed themselves to a constitutional monarchy found themselves marked men. As the latter began to flee abroad, the aristocratic Parisian high society which had survived 1789 came to an end.

August the 10th had been a blow to the Legislative Assembly, which not only was obliged to suspend Louis XVI, but also had to accept the demands of Robespierre and the *sans culottes* for the election of a new Assembly, the Convention, by universal suffrage. However, the new Assembly would be faced with a formidable rival in the shape of an enlarged Paris Commune, which had replaced the old *bourgeois* municipal authority and taken control of the National Guard and the police, both recruited on a broader social basis from the former 'passive' citizens. Because of its intimate connection with the *sans culottes* of the sections, the insurrectionary Commune was able to challenge the authority of the Assembly in the capital; furthermore, it began to send commissioners to the provinces and the army as part of its strategy of radicalising the Revolution. The dethronement of the king and the final clearing away of aristocratic privilege led directly to the triumph of political equality and direct democracy in Paris, based firmly on the victory of the *sans culottes*. 'Passive citizens', those lacking the franchise under the Constitution of 1791, were now admitted to the meetings of the forty-eight *sections,* which assumed responsibility for court and police duties and the hounding of counter-revolutionaries. Successful pressure on the Assembly to abolish remaining feudal dues and to inaugurate the sale of *émigré* property was designed to ensure the support of the provincial rural population (**22**, book iii, ch. 3).

The origins of the second revolution of August 1792 can be traced to the flight of the king to Varennes on 21 June 1791. The king increasingly saw the work of the Constituent Assembly as a merely provisional solution and hoped that, with foreign assistance, he could create a new regime based on the programme he had outlined to the States-General in 1789. Although he was influenced by the strongly anti-revolutionary views of the queen and his sister, Madame Elisabeth, the civil constitution of the clergy in 1790 was more important in stiffening his unwillingness to cooperate in the constitutional experiment. Indeed, it had the same effect on many other people. The early months of 1790 were a period of general social calm, despite sporadic peasant revolts and clashes between government officials and local factions in provincial towns. Only in Nîmes in the south-east was there anything like a major confrontation between the forces of revolution and counter-revolution. Here the Revolution brought to the boil hostility between Catholics and Calvinist Protestants, which remained as a legacy of bloody conflict from the Reformation to the end of the Seven Years War in 1763 (**92**). In most parts of France, however, even the prosperous classes were willing for the moment to suppress their anxieties about the common people and hope that the king and the nobility would accept the principles of 1789.

Events in Nîmes, displaying the power of religion to divide men, were an ill omen. The civil constitution of the clergy undermined the basic consensus of early 1790; henceforth religion began its march to stand at the side of counter-revolution. Attacks on churches and priests in parts of the provinces, many of them spontaneous and 'unofficial', laid open old scars of confessional hatreds and inflicted new ones. Religion was not however, the only cause of social and political divisions which made more difficult the task of men like Mirabeau, Barnave, Duport and the Lameth brothers, who were trying to make the monarchy work.

During the spring of 1791 new fraternal and popular societies in Paris joined the Cordeliers Club and the radical press in bringing the lower groups of the capital, the *menu peuple*, into the political orbit. Consequently, the fears of the deputies and 'comfortable bourgeois' for their property rights increased. At the other political extreme, there were courtiers who urged the king to force a crisis and *émigrés* who plotted to restore the *ancien régime*, some of them linked to counter-revolutionary groups in south-east France **(95)**. From late 1790, under pressure from royalists, the king began more seriously to encourage foreign intervention as an instrument for amending the constitution. The king's flight and forcible return to Paris in June 1791 created an immense wave of antimonarchical feeling and widespread fear that an invasion of France was imminent. Although the Assembly refused to depose him – he was merely 'temporarily suspended' – the fact that the king had left behind a document damning many of the acts of the Assembly which he had accepted at the time, served only to compromise him further and cast permanent doubt on his sincerity. Both popular societies and the left-wing press vociferously demanded the king's abdication and trial in what was to prove very much a dress rehearsal for the events of July and August 1792 **(96**, chs 1-4).

The flight to Varennes deepened political and social divisions, for the Assembly, full of moderates, and the municipality, in the hands of prosperous bourgeois from the western districts of the capital, rejected popular demands to arm the people and begin a purge of suspects and counter-revolutionaries. Popular frustration sought an outlet in the growing number of political clubs and acts of hostility towards priests. The prestige of the Assembly sank with that of the king, for the *menu peuple* had not forgotten Duport's remarks on 17 May that 'the Revolution is over. It is necessary to stabilize it and preserve it by combatting extremism. Equality must be restrained, liberty reduced and opinion controlled.' While Duport and his colleagues seceded from the Jacobin Club and formed the Feuillant Club, committed to a policy of cooperation with the discredited monarch, the conservative municipality took firm action against the popular movement **(88**, ch. 10). On 17 July it attacked a crowd gathered on the Champ de Mars to sign a petition for the dethronement of the king. About fifty were killed (**71**, ch.6; **96**, ch.6). Thus the divisions within the third estate were openly revealed; no longer could it be presented as a united front against the aristocracy. The small masters and wage-earners of the capital appeared, under the leadership of the Cordeliers and Jacobin Clubs, as an element in the Revolution which could not be ignored [**doc.6**]. There was now a clear line between those who sought compromise and more or less agreed with the words of Duport on the 17 May, and those who did not. Many men who had been 'patriots' in 1789 now found themselves pushed, by the growing popular movement in Paris and fears for their wealth and property, to the side of the monarchy and the Feuillants, thus becoming heirs of the *monarchiens* whom they had despised two years earlier. The alliance of differing social groups which had carried through the revolution of 1789 now disappeared.

The search for stability by Barnave and the moderate Feuillants, on the basis of a revived constitutional monarchy, was doomed to failure. Neither the royalists of the extreme right nor Robespierre, Pétion and the revolutionary democrats would offer any assistance. Although the king publicly accepted the Constitution of 1791 (described by the queen in a private letter as 'monstrous'), it had little appeal for the Parisian popular movement, resting as it did on a restricted franchise. Neither did it attract many noble deputies, who voted against it with their feet by fleeing to the frontier and joining the earlier *émigrés*. The greatest blow to the constitution was struck by the king himself when he vetoed the November decrees against the non-juring clergy.

Increasingly the running in the Legislative Assembly was made by the Girondins, or Brissotins, a loosely-knit group of deputies, the core of whom came from the Gironde region (**99**). Not only did they seek ministerial office for themselves, but they also launched attacks on priests and *émigrés* as part of their strategy to push France into war against the wishes of the Feuillants and democrats like Robespierre who saw war as a royalist and counter-revolutionary trap. War, claimed Brissot and the powerful Girondin press, would bring the Revolution to a climax, unmask counter-revolutionaries, intriguing courtiers and ministers, bring economic prosperity (it was assumed the war would be short and successful) and unite Frenchmen in defence of *la patrie*. The king and the royalists also favoured hostilities, though for very different reasons from the Girondins. War, they hoped, would put the Revolution into reverse and restore royal and aristocratic authority. The new emperor, Francis II, was more willing to go to war than his predecessor. Moreover, a growing bellicose popular feeling in the winter of 1791-92 deepened the expectation of hostilities. This feeling was a byproduct of popular revolutionary fervour and fear of counter-revolution within France. Early in 1792 a young student wrote to his father 'our liberty can only be assured in so far as it has a mattress of corpses on its bed. . . I am willing to become one of these corpses'. Such heroic delirium became more common and reached a climax in the *'vaincre ou mourir'* patriotism of the *fédérés* in the summer. A preoccupation with blood, death and sacrifice was an essential ingredient of the popular revolutionary mentality and is linked to the social psychology of the Terror.

War became a certainty when the king appointed a 'Patriot' Girondin ministry in March and it was declared on the emperor on 20 April 1792, being destined to last twenty-three years. In the words of Professor Reinhard, 'war revolutionised the Revolution'. It deepened the gulf between moderates and extremists that had appeared at the time of Varennes. It made the Revolution international and hence more extreme under attack by the crowned heads of Europe; extreme measures were deemed necessary for survival. It intensified irrational fears and panics: that, for example, traitors lurked around every corner ready to deliver the Revolution into the hands of its foreign enemies, linked to armies of brigands, counter-revolutionaries and Austrians, who were allegedly concealed in the quarries beneath Paris, ready at a signal to emerge and seize the city **(97)**. Such fears were lent some credence by counter-revolutionary outbreaks in the Ardèche and Brittany. Those who seemed in any way 'moderate' and antidemocratic were equated with traitors as 'enemies of the people'. Such views were characteristic of the *sans culottes*, whom war pushed further into prominence. An army weakened by unreliable officers and undisciplined ranks would have to rely increasingly on volunteers from the urban working population; in return the *sans culottes* would demand an increased voice in policy-making. This would swing the Revolution sharply to the left.

The *sans culottes* were also motivated by economic grievances. The harvest of 1791 was mediocre and grain prices rose quickly in winter. Civil war in the West Indies created a serious shortage of sugar, a shortage aggravated by speculators. In January and February 1792 there was widespread pillaging of shops and warehouses for sugar and coffee, followed by *sans culotte* demands that free trade in grain, sacred to the liberal bourgeoisie, be abandoned, that prices be fixed by law and rigorous measures taken against food hoarders, speculators, rich merchants and prosperous rural proprietors. Peasants in a number of country areas attacked *châteaux* and seized and divided common land. High prices, insisted the *sans culottes*, were counter-revolutionary and deliberately designed to sustain the *pacte de famine* and starve the common people into submission. This economic crisis led to further social rupture, with members of popular clubs and societies adopting the *bonnet rouge* and castigating the *honnête gens* — the comfortably-off bourgeois. The rich *messieurs*, as opposed to poor *citoyens*, were viewed, like moderate politicians, as the catspaws of counter-revolution (**96**, ch. 13; **71**, ch. 7).

War brought not only inflation and economic hardship, but also military defeat. The *sans culottes* and democratic leaders like Marat put this down to treacherous generals, the king and his court. Not long after the outbreak of war, the king and his ministers were being sneeringly referred to as 'the Austrian committee', whilst commanders like Lafayette were accused of being more concerned to defeat the Parisian democratic movement than the enemy armies. Neither accusation was wide of the mark. Anger against the monarchy, which had smouldered among the democrats and *menu peuple* since the flight to Varennes, blazed up again when the king dismissed the Girondin ministry and vetoed more laws against priests. On 20 June an armed crowd gained entrance to the Tuileries, shouting *'A bas le veto!'*, and forced Louis to don the red cap of liberty and drink the health of the nation, though he refused to withdraw his veto. The crowd was persuaded to leave quietly and there was no bloodshed.

On 3 August the crisis deepened further when the Brunswick Manifesto was published. Written in fact by an *émigré* associate of Fersen, the queen's devoted admirer, it expressed the desires and instructions of the French royal family, although it purported to come from the Prussian commander. The declaration that National Guards would be regarded as outside the laws of war, and shot by the invading Prussians if caught bearing arms, stung Paris to intense fury. A wave of patriotism and renewed hostility towards the king swept many moderates along with it, for they had no desire to see their newfound wealth go back into the hands of the *émigrés* in the allied baggage train. Hence the National Guard, which had recently recruited 'passive' citizens, was seriously divided and the forces of order in Paris weakened, as they had been in July 1789. The Legislative Assembly, torn by a complex series of clashes and intrigues between Girondins, Jacobins, followers of Lafayette and Feuillants, was paralysed into inaction as petitions came flooding in demanding the overthrow of the king and the arming of the people. It was in this situation of extreme crisis that the *fédérés* and *sans culottes* in the Paris sections continued to fraternise and combine into the powerful force which attacked the Tuileries on 10 August and brought about the downfall of the monarchy and, soon afterwards, the declaration of a Republic.

SANS CULOTTES

The great *journée* of 10 August 1792 had brought the *sans culottes* to the forefront of the Revolution. Not only had they been instrumental in the overthrow of the monarchy, but the opening of the assemblies of the forty-eight sections of Paris to 'passive' citizens gave them a secure political base for their growing influence on the course of the Revolution, an influence which was to reach its peak between June and December 1793, when they shared with the Revolutionary government the administration of France and the direction of the Terror. Until fairly recently the *sans culottes* were either neglected by historians or misleadingly depicted as an urban proletariat, valiantly resisting hard-faced capitalism. In 1958, however, Albert Soboul published his vast thesis which analyses the Parisian *sans culottes* in clinical detail, while Richard Cobb has provided a great deal of evidence for provincial *sans culotterie*. (**102, 103, 104, 106**)

It is clear that the *sans culottes* did not form an economic class, but were made up of a combination of socially disparate elements. Those who called themselves *sans culottes* ranged from wage-earners at the bottom to men at the top like Santerre, the wealthy brewer; Duplay, the 'cabinet maker' and Robespierre's landlord, who was in fact a large scale furniture contractor and drew 10-12,000 *livres* a year from rents alone; Lefranc the 'carpenter', who was in reality a prosperous building contractor who employed two hundred workmen. Revolutionary fervour caused many wealthy men to 'democratise' their occupations on paper (**108**). Yet the bulk of the Parisian *sans culottes* were tradesmen, shop-keepers, craftsmen, small masters, *compagnons* and journeymen, accurately reflecting the economic structure of Paris industry, where large factories were rare and the average master employed between four and fourteen *garçons*. Shopkeepers, wine merchants, petty clerks and former professional soldiers were especially prominent among the militants. It should be stressed that these militants were a minority. Members of *sociétés populaires* were less than five per cent of the adult population of their surrounding areas, while actual attendance was confined to between four and nineteen per cent of the members in Paris (**108, 107** ch. 2). They did not include many from the very bottom of society, for criminals, beggars, casual labourers and *gens sans aveu* tended to be apathetic or even counter-revolutionary. The *'pauvre bougre'* was not relatively all that poor in normal times, although in the Years II and III he was pushed by dearth and food shortage to the brink of starvation (**106**, section iii, part 2).

Because the *sans culottes* included so many employers of labour, most of them admittedly on a small scale, they never developed a coherent

51

economic policy clearly distinguished from that of the *bourgeoisie.* They did not oppose wealth and property as such, only 'large' property *(gros possédants)* and 'excessive' wealth. Combinations of wage-earners tended to be regarded as inimical to the war effort. Small property and carefully husbanded modest wealth were seen as virtuous, despite such phrases in petitions as 'selfish rich', 'idle rich' and 'useless rich' **(102, ch. 1).** Masters and men, living and working together, were too closely bound for a clear distinction and antagonism to appear between capital and labour. Social divisions were arranged vertically in the storeys of tenement buildings, rather than horizontally in suburbs and working-class districts. Like the peasantry, the *sans culottes* saw their economic ideal in the past rather than in any future socialist utopia. They aspired to a traditional society of small independent producers, whom the state would sustain by taxing the very rich and restricting the operation of *laissez-faire* and large scale capitalism. This outlook was partly caused by the fear of many independent craftsmen that they might be sucked down into the ranks of a wage-earning and dependent proletariat [**doc.12**].

Sans culotte was something of a portmanteau expression. It denoted a moral and political category as much as, perhaps more than, an economic one. The *bon sans culotte* regarded himself as a superior moral being and the epitome of Republican virtue [**doc.10**]. Manual labour itself was regarded as almost sacred. In his barely-furnished garret, the good *sans culotte* was a hard working, honest, humble and rather priggishly puritan citizen, who was essentially urban and saw the country-side as bringing up the somewhat reluctant rearguard of the Revolution. He was a good husband and family man, who saw women's place as in the home and who named his children after heroes like Brutus or William Tell, rather than the saints; when he ran out of heroes' names, he turned to those of flowers and trees, fruit and fish. Sometimes he changed his own name; Professor Cobb observes that 'the list of the members of the *société populaire* of Perpignan reads like a seedsman's catalogue' **(108).** There was always a humourless and rather ridiculous strain among the militants. The *sans culotte* looked askance at prostitutes, classified as counter-revolutionary survivals from the decadent *ancien régime.* Bachelors were regarded as hedonistic evaders of family responsibilities. Cards, billiards, fancy dress and carnivals were opposed as undesirable and frivolous distractions from toil and political duties. The only permissible outlet was swearing and drinking; *sans culottes* loved to hold forth in the cabarets and much of the disorder characteristic of the sectional assemblies was a result of cheap wine on undernourished stomachs. According to the *Père Duchesne,* to drink water was a crime.

The ideal *sans culotte,* depicted in popular prints, wore his hair long, smoked a pipe and dressed simply: cotton trousers (rather than the knee-breeches, *culottes,* of the aristocracy and bourgeoisie), a short jacket and the *bonnet rouge* (the Phrygian cap of the freed slave in ancient times). Powdered wigs, scent, knee-breeches, buckled shoes, flowered waistcoats, bows and lorgnettes were dismissed as foppish and frivolous trappings of privilege, with overtones of sexual deviancy. Equally dismissed were the manners and deferent behaviour of the *ancien régime:* the good *sans culotte* took his hat off to nobody, used the familiar 'tu' rather than 'vous' and 'citoyen' rather than 'monsieur', and swore in the colourful Parisian slang of the *Père Duchesne.* He tended to judge enemies by their appearance: those who wore fancy clothes, spoke in 'posh' tones, looked haughty, or failed to offer the fraternal kiss of liberty. Those who seemed to despise the honest working man were in trouble. A music dealer was arrested as a suspect for observing, at a sectional meeting, 'It was disgusting to see a cobbler acting as president, particularly a cobbler who was badly dressed' (**102,** chs 1 and 6).

'Aristocrat' and 'moderate' became interchangeable terms for those who opposed in any way the outlook and aspirations of the *sans culottes* or appeared to look down on them or ridicule them; they were also applied to those who seemed indifferent and lacking in the open enthusiasm of the good revolutionary. 'Aristocrat' could include those who refused to buy *biens nationaux* or to cultivate land or sell it at a fair price, or failed to find employment for labourers and journeymen, or refused to subscribe generously to patriotic loans, or to those who dealt in gold rather than republican *assignats* or speculated on the *Bourse* or in joint stock companies [**doc. 11**]. As the revolutionary crisis deepened in 1793, 'aristocrat' increasingly came to mean bourgeois property owner; in May an orator in the Section du Mail declared: 'Aristocrats are the rich wealthy merchants, monopolists, middlemen, bankers, trading clerks, quibbling lawyers and citizens who own anything.' Wealth always raised *sans culotte* suspicion, unless offset by outstanding political virtue. Hoarders and monopolists were seen as hand-in-glove with large merchants, bankers and economic liberals in a plot to starve the people and crush the Revolution; for *sans culottes* were ultra sensitive to the problem of food supply and the price of bread, while they lived in constant fear of plots and betrayal. Hunger, as well as democratic politics and puritanical moral views, was a cement holding the disparate *sans culotte* groups together. Hence pillage could be justified as 'egalitarian' and 'revolutionary', in that it fed the people and struck at the machinations of hoarders and speculators, the visible vanguard of counter-revolution. *Sans culottes* always tended to advocate immediate and violent political solutions to economic problems and, with brutal simplicity, assumed that spilling blood would provide bread (**104**, i, ch. 3).

Despite the fact that many *sans culottes* were small property owners, there existed a deep-rooted egalitarianism. They believed in the 'right to live' (*'droit à l'existence'*) and in 'the equality of the benefits of society' (*l'égalité des jouissances*) (**102**, ch. 2). A family should have enough to live on in modest comfort, especially sufficient bread of good quality flour. No rich man should have the power of life and death over his fellow men by his ability to monopolise food and other basic necessities [**doc. 12**]. Thus food prices and distribution should be controlled by law, while the government should take stern action against hoarders and speculators. Some of the more radical *sans culotte* committees demanded taxation of the rich, limitation of rents, restriction of the activities of large financiers, government-assisted workshops and allowances for widows, orphans and disabled soldiers.

Although the *sans culottes* despised 'intellectuals' and the 'useless' privileged learning and arts of the *ancien régime*, they were very self-conscious of their own lack of education and illiteracy. They often therefore ran schools to inculcate what they regarded as a 'useful' revolutionary education, more moral than intellectual, among the young revolutionary generation. Young children sang their *Marseillaise* and revolutionary hymns, danced the *Carmagnole* and parroted the Declaration of the Rights of Man. Some were even taken to public executions as part of their civic education. Such expressions of fervour were linked to the patriotic chauvinism of the *sans culottes*. They were fully committed to the war and indeed many of them had jobs in the war machine. Early universalism and a desire to spread the Revolution abroad soon evaporated when foreigners proved unwilling to turn on their rulers. When France herself came under the threat of invasion, *sans culotte* hatred for the foreigner asserted itself. Cosmopolitanism of any kind became sinful. Even dialects and languages like Breton were condemned as unpatriotic. By its very nature, *sans culotterie* was French and localised; no attempts were made to forge links with foreign artisans and revolutionaries; indeed, to make such links between French cities was difficult enough.

'*Sans culotte*' was also a political expression, born of accident and emergency in 1792. Even a rich man could be a *sans culotte* if he had a good political record, above all if he had participated in the great revolutionary *journées* like the Bastille, the Champ de Mars or 10 August. The *sans culotte* regarded such *journées* as a legitimate expression of popular sovereignty. He was a fervent believer in direct democracy, a concept which stemmed ultimately from Rousseau and the *Social Contract* and filtered down into the sections through the revolutionary press, broadsheets and speeches, revolutionary songs and Jacobin Club pamphlets and propaganda. Authority could not be delegated, for the true basis of government was the people, sitting permanently in their evening sectional meetings, where they discussed laws and decrees. Deputies should be delegates rather than representatives and be constantly and immediately answerable to the *sociétés populaires*. The latter had the right to scrutinise the laws of the Assembly, administer justice and the police, and help to run the war effort. Thus the *sans culottes* saw themselves and the 'nation' as synonymous.

A government defied the 'nation' at its peril, for the *sans culottes* insisted on the right to bear arms, especially the 'sacred pike', and overthrow an 'illegitimate' government by force. In such an insurrection the tocsin would be rung, the drums beat, the warning cannon fire and the people be flushed with excitement as they brought their influence to bear on the very centre of power. Secrecy of any kind in government was regarded as counter-revolutionary, for plots were hatched in secret. All meetings of the legislative and administrative bodies should be held in public; all decisions should be open and vocal; secret ballots were furtive and undignified.

Not only should politics be open, and therefore constantly vulnerable to popular pressure, they should also be unanimous. Unity was necessary to defeat the internal and external enemies of the Revolution. Those who were not enthusiastically in favour of the popular Revolution must necessarily be against it. Dissent was intolerable, for the *sans culottes* cared nothing for individualism or the rights of minorities; as Soboul puts it; 'the *sans culotte* did not think of himself as an isolated individual: he thought and acted *en masse*' (**102**, ch. 4). Constant vigilance was necessary to spot counter-revolutionaries and those who dragged their feet. The informer and denouncer was not odious, but performing his sincere and patriotic civic duty in rooting out suspects and sending them to the guillotine: the 'people's axe', the 'national hatchet', the 'scythe of equality' [**doc. 14**].

Very many *sans culottes* were simple and credulous men who saw issues in the extreme black and white terms of the uneducated. In periods of calm many of them were indifferent and did not bother to turn up for meetings, except when they needed their *certificats de civisme* as passports to jobs and allowances. However, such calm periods became rarer after late 1792, when the country was threatened with invasion, hunger and counter-revolution. At such a time, gnawed by hunger and excited by alarm bells and cannon fire, the *sans culottes* could dramatise themselves in heady rhetoric, embrace and weep tears of joy over their heroes and friends, and brutally hack their enemies to pieces with butchers' knives. Their excitability, gullibility, conceit, deprivation, suspicion of plots and betrayal, of moderates, rich men and priests were to provide the fuel for the engine of the great Terror of 1793-94.

THE FIRST TERROR

After the downfall of the monarchy on 10 August 1792 the *sans culottes* and the Paris Commune demanded immediate and decisive action against hoarders, speculators, priests and suspected counter-revolutionaries, as the war crisis mounted daily. During the six weeks before the end of the Legislative Assembly, the legal authority of the Assembly came into conflict with the 'revolutionary' power of the insurrectionary Commune, a conflict pregnant for the future course of the Revolution. The *vainqueurs* of the Tuileries sought to impose their will on an Assembly which resented the threatening tone of the Commune and was conscious that Paris was not the whole nation. Both Commune and Assembly took haphazard and sometimes conflicting decisions in the confused situation. When the Assembly sent twelve members to the armies at the frontier, with power to dismiss generals and officers, the Commune sent commissioners to the departments to rally support for purges of local government officials, the arrest of suspects and the creation of committees of *surveillance* (110).

On 17 August, in order to rally the petty *bourgeois* and urban masses, the Assembly gave way to some of the demands of the Commune and put the First Terror into operation by creating an extraordinary criminal tribunal, whose judges were elected by the Paris sections, to try those suspected of 'counter-revolutionary crimes'. On 28 August a major step was taken in the erection of the apparatus of Terror when domiciliary visits were authorised in order to search for arms and suspects. Municipalities were ordered to root out counter-revolutionaries, whilst officials and priests had to swear an oath of liberty and equality. Priests who failed to take the oath were given fifteen days to flee the country or be sent to the 'dry guillotine' of Guiana. Feudal dues were abolished where the landlord could not produce the original title; lands of *émigrés* were to be sold in small lots; births, marriages and deaths were subject to civil registration, for the last remaining religious congregations were abolished. However, the Assembly drew a line at harsh measures against hoarders and refused to make general the price-fixing adopted by some local authorities.

Meanwhile the military situation was deteriorating. What had begun as a war of liberation was turning into a desperate struggle for survival. On 26 August news arrived in Paris of the fall of Longwy, as well as an attempted insurrection in La Vendée. The enemy seemed everywhere. In an atmosphere of crisis and alarm, the Commune took the lead in organising the defence of the capital. Over 30,000 pikes were manufactured; arms were taken from suspects and given to the *menu peuple,* by 2 September there were about 2,800 suspects imprisoned in the capital. On 1 September news came that the enemy were besieging traitor-ridden Verdun, the last fortress blocking the road to Paris. The Commune now proclaimed 'To arms citizens, the enemy is at our gates!. The tocsin sounded, barriers were erected and during the next three weeks over 20,000 volunteers left the capital to defend the Revolution.

In this tense atmosphere fear of treason increased. A rumour spread that, as the volunteers left, so imprisoned suspects would break out and hand the city over to the enemy. Marat warned volunteers not to leave their wives and families before bringing the enemies of the people to justice. On the afternoon óf 2 September the First Terror rose to its climax, when a band of *gardes, fédérés* and Bretons put to death a group of refractory priests they were escorting to gaol. Then prisons, monasteries and seminaries were attacked by a crowd of shopkeepers, artisans, *fédérés* and national guards in a series of bloody massacres which lasted until 7 September. According to Pierre Caron, about 1,300 prisoners were killed, 67 per cent of them in prison for non-political offences (111). The September Massacres shocked Europe, especially revolutionary sympathisers in Britain, and repelled many educated and moderate revolutionaries in France. But they were applauded by the *sans culottes* as a necessary act of patriotic vengeance against traitors, plotters and counterfeiters who sent up the cost of living. They saw the slaughter as a measure of public health, a perfectly 'legal' reprisal for the killing of *sans culottes* at the front through treachery and at the Tuileries by mercenaries (107, ch. 2; 17, ch. 8). The authorities were impotent during the crisis and could only turn a blind eye, while the *comité de surveillance* of the Commune, which Marat joined on 2 September, justified its collusion in the massacres as 'this step towards public safety, absolutely necessary to root out by means of Terror the legions of traitors hidden within our walls, ready for the moment when the people march off to face the enemy'. The Commune later compensated the murderers for their loss of earnings while engaged on their grisly task.

The First Terror and the September Massacres showed the face of the new popular democratic Revolution, with its hatred of foreign invaders, aristocrats, priests and prostitutes. Its belief in direct democracy also prompted hatred of what it regarded as a weak middle-class Assembly, based on representative parliamentary government which seemed out-dated to the people of the Paris *sections*. A clumsy attempt by the Assembly to curb the power of the Commune had to be abandoned in face of the imminent invasion crisis. Danton, Minister of Justice, thundered defiance at the foreign armies in a series of powerful speeches calling on the people to show boldness and courage. Arms, horses, fodder and workshops were requisitioned. Women helped the men to barricade the ramparts of the capital and met in the churches to stitch clothing. A nervous bourgeois could do nothing to stem the tide of popular enthusiasm.

In fact the Prussian advance was less formidable than it looked and on 20 September the French cannonade forced the Prussians to retreat at the Battle of Valmy. Victory was gained by French regular troops and the volunteers of 1791, while the Prussian retreat was accelerated by dysentery and torrential rain. Although the volunteers of 1792, untrained and undisciplined, had been kept well to the rear of the French army, the *sans culottes* claimed the victory and spread the potent myth that the Prussians had been beaten by an army of tailors and cobblers whose ignorance of military drill was outweighed by its revolutionary fervour and high morale. That the Revolution has been saved was no myth. Verdun and Longwy were liberated in October; in the following month the Austrians were beaten at Jemappes and the French overran Belgium. France was free from a major threat of invasion until the spring of 1793. No wonder Goethe, on the field at Valmy, felt he had seen the dawn of a new era. Blood, terror and total war had marked the advent of democracy in European history (124, ch. 1).

Events between 10 August and the Battle of Valmy revealed the breakdown of any kind of political compromise solution. The pressures of war and the fear of counter-revolution had undermined the constitution of 1791; the question posed in 1789, how was the state to be run when the *ancien régime* was destroyed?, was thrown open again. In August 1792 the rivalries between the Legislative Assembly, the Paris Commune, the Executive Council of ministers and the general assemblies of the Paris sections had seemed to rob central government of all purpose and direction, a confusion which had been only temporarily disguised by the exigencies of the invasion crisis in early September. Even the election of a National Convention by universal suffrage could not remove the fundamental conflict which had developed since the outbreak of war between the popular and parliamentary versions of democracy, each claiming indivisible sovereignty, each linked to social antagonisms and the conflict between Paris and the provinces.

GIRONDINS AND MONTAGNARDS

The National Convention which assembled on 20 September 1792 was scarcely representative of the nation. Not only had various royalist and moderate groups been disfranchised, but only about a million of an electorate of five million had bothered to vote. Its composition was much the same as its two predecessors: mainly the urban middle class with a preponderance of lawyers. Indeed 96 former members of the Constituent and 190 members of the Legislative were elected. There were only two working men; labouring *sans culottes* were never able to get themselves elected at either national or municipal level. For a brief period there was something of a truce between the warring factions of August. Even the Paris Commune was willing to accept the absolute sovereignty of the Convention for the moment. The monarchy was abolished by unanimous vote, and the declaration of a Republic 'one and indivisible' was passed without dissent; Year I of the Republic commenced on 22 September. Some deputies, influenced by the brief current mood of social fraternity induced by the meeting of the Convention and military victory, began using the *'tu'* form, abandoned the use of *'monsieur'* and forsook powdered wigs and silk breeches for the informal dress of the *sans culottes.*

Such harmony proved to be shortlived. Within a few weeks the Convention was torn apart by the dispute between Girondins and Montagnards, a struggle which lasted until the Girondins were expelled on 2 June 1793. The exact nature of the struggle has caused historical controversy. Were the Girondins and Montagnards tightly organised parties? Was the struggle based on personal rivalries and the desire for place and power, or was it the political manifestation of a social and economic class struggle? While parties in the modern sense did not exist in the Convention, being associated pejoratively with faction and disruption as in eighteenth-century England, most historians would accept that the Montagnards were relatively well organised, in that they were a small group whose tactics had often been concerted in the Jacobin Club, of which they gained complete control in November [doc. 6]. But the view of Lamartine, Michelet and Mathiez, that the Girondins were a coherent party, has been challenged by Professor Sydenham, who sees the idea of a Girondin 'party' as a creation of Montagnard propaganda (99, 101). What loose ties there were between the associates of Brissot were based more on personal friendship and temperament than on any firm organisation or common policy. The final victory of the Montagnards in fact owed a good deal to the disunity of their opponents.

Marxist historians like Soboul, following Mathiez, see the Girondins as the party of wealth, representing the industrialists and high commercial bourgeoisie, while the Montagnards represented the smaller bourgeoisie and the *menu peuple* of artisans and shopkeepers. The policy of the former was designed to satisfy those at the top of society: that of the latter was geared to the needs of the masses (**20**, part ii, ch. 2). This has been challenged by Lefebvre and English historians, including Professor Hampson, who point out that both factions were agreed on the main lines of policy: hatred of privilege, anticlericalism and economic liberalism. Factional rivalries and personal quarrels were more significant (**22**, book iii, ch. 5; **18**, ch. 7). It may be that many Montagnards were more concerned with social welfare than the majority of the deputies, but at bottom their economic ideas were also rooted in liberal doctrine. This is illustrated by the issue of price control and grain circulation. The Convention abandoned the arrangements for requisitioning grain undertaken in August during the invasion crisis. In the autumn, however, there were disturbances in Lyon, where unemployed silk weavers forced the municipality to control the price of basic foodstuffs and tax the rich. These were followed by peasant revolts in the Beauce and the Ile de France, where grain requisitioning for the armies had reduced the supply and raised prices; markets were plundered as peasants demanded price control. Such demands were echoed by the *sans culottes* of the Paris sections. Roland, the Minister of the Interior, argued that price control would mean more violence and even civil war, while neither Robespierre nor Saint-Just would accept price control. Both Montagnards and Girondins wanted the peasants firmly put down and endorsed the policy of free trade in grain and the rejection of price control adopted in December.

When the Convention met the Girondins had some advantages. They commanded a majority in the Assembly, in that most of the deputies were moderate men who were shocked at the September massacres and were suspicious of the Montagnards, the 'men of the Mountain' who sat on benches high on the left of the Convention and were led by Robespierre and the twenty-four Jacobin deputies for Paris. Not only were the Jacobins known to have close links with the *sans culottes* and those accused of anarchy and terror, but the Girondins insisted on the maintenance of the law, the rights of the provinces and the sovereignty of the Convention. Besides standing to profit from the wave of revulsion against the First Terror, the Girondins held a virtual monopoly of ministerial posts. So the initiative seemed to be with the Girondins in the intense quarrel which had originated early in the year when Robespierre had opposed the war the Girondins so badly wanted and later accused the Girondin ministers of being enemies of the people and reluctant to prosecute total war. Antagonism had been exacerbated by the revolution of 10 August, which Robespierre had worked for and which the Girondins had tried to forestall, and the attacks which the Legislative Assembly had launched on the Paris Commune late in August.

The Girondins, partly because of their basic disunity, frittered away some of their advantages. Their attacks on Paris as a centre of anarchy and disorder, their desire to be rid of the extraordinary revolutionary tribunal established in August, their attempts to pin responsibility for the September massacres on the leading Jacobins and the Commune, their stigmatising of Robespierre, Danton and Marat as an aspiring triumvirate dictatorship: each alienated many of the moderate Paris sections which had themselves been shocked by the September massacres and could have been won over. As it was, the frontal assault which the Girondins made on the capital pushed all the sections together behind the Montagnards, who consolidated their domination of Paris by gaining complete control of the Jacobin Club in November. Accusations of 'Parisian anarchy' by the Girondins made it seem that they both feared and despised the masses and regarded only themselves as fit to rule. Unsuccessful Girondin attempts to create a departmental national guard responsible to the Convention as a counter to the military power of the Paris sections, laid them open to the charge of 'federalism', though none of them actually ever argued for a federal republic. Unconcerted attacks on Paris and on the Jacobin leaders tended to have little positive result in the face of Montagnard obstruction while alienating relatively uncommitted deputies who saw the supposed party of order apparently indulging in prolonged personal vindictiveness which led to political stalemate rather than progress in the essential tasks of government. Increasingly unpopular were the naked party ambitions of the Girondins, who aimed at installing themselves in all positions of authority. Many came to feel that only the Montagnards could supply the Revolution with a clear sense of direction.

By late November the Montagnards, assisted by the growing power of the Jacobin Club and pressure from the *sans culottes* in the public gallery of the Convention, were more confident and made their influence felt beyond their relatively small numbers. The gulf between the two sides was irrevocably deepened by the trial and execution of the king. Demands for his trial had existed among the people of Paris since before 10 August; they saw him as guilty of the deaths of many of their number; in the words of Saint-Just: 'He is the murderer of the people at the Bastille, at Nancy, on the Champ de Mars, at Tournay, at the Tuileries: what enemy, what foreigner, has done you more harm?' Louis was clearly guilty of the charge of encouraging counter-revolution:

proof was furnished in November when the secret 'iron cupboard' in the Tuileries containing the king's correspondence was discovered. To defend the king would be to condemn the revolution of 10 August. Yet there was considerable reluctance to send him to the guillotine; not only would his martyrdom encourage royalist counter-revolution among those already alienated by attacks on churches and priests, but to destroy divine monarchy with a steel blade was certain to widen and intensify the war and risk another crisis like that of August and another terror to accompany it.

Debate on the fate of the king began on 13 November and lasted two months. It was here that the icy, terrifyingly abstract Saint-Just, at barely twenty-five the youngest member of the Convention, made his mark on the Revolution. The king, he alleged, did not deserve a trial, for royalty itself was a crime and the king should die for being what he was, rather than for what he had done. Robespierre supported this cold terrorist logic by arguing that the Republic could never be stable while Louis was alive. The Girondins were badly divided on the issue, as on most issues, and lost the initiative to the Montagnards in what was essentially a struggle for leadership of the Convention (**99**, appendix C). Those of them who tried to save the king by calling for a national referendum exposed themselves to charges of royalism and reaction, charges which the Montagnards were quick to pin indiscriminately on all their opponents. Robespierre, who argued that the people had already conducted a referendum on 10 August, managed to secure a system of verbal open voting by rote which, allied with intense pressure from Parisian democrats, secured a majority of 53 for the death of the king (**124**, ch. 2).

On 21 January 1793 Louis XVI was beheaded amidst the noise of rolling drums. Terror and rule by a dedicated minority were implicit in his execution by a small majority of an unrepresentative parliament. Once again the Revolution had swung in a more extreme direction; compromise with moderates inside France or with governments beyond the frontiers was henceforth remote. Lebas, deputy for the Pas de Calais, wrote on 20 January: 'The roads behind us have been destroyed, we must go forward, willingly or unwillingly; the issue now is whether to live in freedom or die.'

6   Anarchic Terror 1793

CRISIS OF THE REVOLUTION
Immediately after the execution of the king the Revolution was faced
with a massive crisis involving military defeat, widespread counter-
revolutionary rebellion, economic troubles and *sans culotte* discontent.
This crisis brought the conflict between the Girondins and the
Montagnards to a climax in two great *journées* on 31 May and 2 June
which swept away Girondin influence and inaugurated what Marat
called 'the despotism of liberty': the attempt to save the Revolution by
force and Terror.

The war had been extended and peace made increasingly remote by
the opening of the Scheldt, the edict of fraternity, the exploitation of
Belgium and the execution of Louis XVI. In February and March France
went to war with England, Holland and Spain, thus taking on the
three great European maritime powers as well as the two major territorial
powers; she now aimed at the newly invented 'natural frontiers' of the
Alps and the Rhine. Such expansionary plans were dealt a sharp blow
in March, when Dumouriez was beaten in Holland and Belgium flared in
revolt. The outbreak of rebellion in La Vendée in the same month put
the Republic in deadly peril. Yet the central government was weak in
the face of a crisis of such magnitude. Political disunity was more rife
than ever, and strong executive power was still distrusted. Obstruction
by the vigorous Montagnard minority made firm and efficient government impossible. As time went on and the crisis deepened, it became
clear that new, powerful organs of executive government were necessary
to deal with it.

Not only were there threats to the government from the frontiers
and provinces, there was also mounting discontent in Paris, for high
bread prices and unemployment had driven hordes of the hungry to the
capital in search of work. Inflation, a result of the large numbers of
assignats issued to finance the war, pushed up prices. Early in 1793 the
cost of a wide range of consumer goods increased rapidly. Soap, for
example, essential for the work of thousands of laundry women, had
reached 23-28 *sous,* compared with 12 *sous* in 1790 **(113)**. On 25 and
26 February grocers' and chandlers' shops were raided by market

women *(dames de la Halle)* who sold goods off at what they considered to be a fair price, although there was also a considerable amount of pillaging. This agitation owed little to the Montagnards. Much of the impetus came from women who were having difficulty keeping a family **(117)**. Robespierre rather sniffily criticized the *menu peuple* for being more concerned with 'vulgar groceries' than the power struggle in the Convention, but he never went short of a meal. Marat, an advocate of speedy revolutionary justice against hoarders and speculators, became the *sans culotte* hero **(174**, ch. 6).

For a brief period, the *enragés* came into prominence with a programme of control of grain prices as a preliminary to a general maximum, the establishment of the *assignat* as sole legal tender, a purge of the army and civil service and general repression of counter-revolution. The *enragés* never amounted to any kind of organized party, for there were no more than a handful of them, despite government propaganda exaggerating their numbers. Jacques Roux, the most prominent of them, is one of the most attractive characters of the Revolution. A priest in one of the Paris sections, he was genuinely appalled by the poverty and hardship of the common people, worse than before 1789. Lacking all personal ambition and political skill, he wanted something done about *la vie chère* **(116**, ch. 10). In fact the *enragé* programme was no different from that of the delegation from the extreme *sans culotte* sections which appeared in the Convention on 12 February and attacked the freedom of the grain trade: 'It is not enough to say that we are French Republicans; it remains necessary for the people to be happy; they must have bread; for when there is no bread, there is no more law, no more liberty, no more Republic.'

Such demands widened the gulf between the Convention and the Paris sections, for the Assembly was firmly against the control of grain prices, as indeed were most members of the Paris Commune. But *sans culottes* tended to put sole blame on the Girondins for resistance to economic controls, even though the Montagnards were no more favourably disposed. On 9 March, the day news of the revolt in Belgium reached Paris, an insurrection was attempted by Varlet, the other leading *enragé,* but came to little apart from the destruction of Girondin printing presses. Neither the Jacobins nor the Commune were yet willing to take drastic action against the Convention; only one or two sections came out in support of Varlet. On 18 March came news of the defeat of Dumouriez at Neerwinden, followed by his desertion to the enemy after an abortive attempt to march on Paris and restore the monarchy and the constitution of 1791. By this time the Vendéan revolt had spread through 600 villages and captured most of the towns in the region.

In such a desperate situation, the Convention was obliged to take drastic measures to reinforce the power of the central government: measures which amounted to the inauguration of the Terror. Eighty-two deputies were sent to the provinces as *représentants en mission,* with wide powers of coercion to secure the implementation of the law of February for the recruitment of 300,000 men. Commissioners were also despatched to the armies to strengthen 'patriotism', by sacking generals and officers if necessary. A Revolutionary tribunal was set up in Paris to deal with counter-revolutionary offences. All rebels captured bearing arms faced the death penalty after summary trial. *Comités de surveillance* were created in all communes and the sections of large towns, initially to keep an eye on the activities of foreigners, but soon assuming police authority for counter-revolutionary offences. In such an atmosphere of crisis the Girondins had no hope of realising their ambitions to 'stabilize' the Revolution. Further measures soon followed. *Émigrés* returning to France with the allied armies or counter-revolutionary bands were threatened with the death penalty. *Émigré* property was to be confiscated. On 6 April the Committee of Public Safety was created to supervise all branches of the executive and to coordinate policy, although it moved cautiously at first. Girondins protested at all this 'dictatorship', but Marat replied: 'Liberty must be established by violence, and the moment has come for the temporary organization of the despotism of liberty, to destroy the despotism of kings' (**174**, ch. 5).

The emergency measures of the spring of 1793 were not taken merely because of defeat across the frontier. In mid-March the great rebellion began in the Vendée when, in Aulard's phrase, the Republic was 'stabbed in the back'. Armed rebellion on a massive scale covered four departments, the most persistent support coming from Maine-et-Loire rather than the department of the Vendée. The rebellion exploded at the end of four years of smouldering tension and antagonism (**118**). Aimed ostensibly at resisting the conscription law of February, the revolt was largely the result of conflict within a backward area of France which had been undergoing rapid social and economic change in the closing years of the *ancien régime.* The heartland of the rebellion was the *bocage,* an area of hedge-enclosed fields, narrow sunken roads and dispersed villages and hamlets. Here backward subsistence agriculture was carried on in a region where nobles possessed large holdings, where the 'feudal' regime of pre-1789 was less resented than in eastern France, and where traditional religious loyalty was (and is) very strong.

Conflict within the region stemmed from the fact that it was not completely rural. Economic change before 1789 had been spearheaded by a bourgeoisie which had established itself in the towns in the area and challenged the nobility for ownership of the land. They had also strengthened their grip on the linen textile industry; as merchants and clothiers they controlled the livelihood of the domestic weavers in the *bocage*. On both counts they were resented as interlopers and usurpers. Nobles, peasants, artisans and clergy regarded the commercial middle class as aliens, undermining the foundations of a traditional and hierarchical society. Hence the revolt took the form of attacking and devastating towns and *bourgs* in the region. At the time of the outbreak of the Revolution, the linen industry was suffering a depression, which deepened after 1789 and caused high unemployment among the artisan weavers, as well as acid resentment of the commercial bourgeoisie. To people in the western countryside, the Revolution seemed very much an urban, bourgeois affair, bringing little benefit to themselves **(119)**. To weavers it seemed to remove tolerable feudal dues but replace them with revolutionary taxation, as well as taking poor relief from the Church and giving it to parsimonious revolutionary committees; to nobles it brought an unwelcome growth in the power of the bourgeoisie in local government and cultural life; to the clergy it brought the sale of Church lands, which reduced their income, lands which tended to end up in bourgeois hands **(93, chs 6 to 9)**.

Revolutionary legislation on the Church in 1790 and 1791 brought antagonism to a head and led to numerous local disturbances and acts of violence. Nowhere were the 'constitutional' priests more harassed, stoned, beaten up and generally resented than in the rural areas of the west. It was the religious issue which politicised the region and created two parties: the 'Patriots' in the towns and valleys, and the 'Aristocrats' in the villages and hamlets of the *bocage*. To ask for peasant and artisan volunteers to fight for a Republic which had attacked the Church and executed the king, besides appearing as the instrument of expanding bourgeois power, seemed the last straw. On 11 March the tocsin rang in 600 villages, calling peasants and textile workers to take up arms in defence of the 'Good Priests' and Louis XVII; to defend the old order against the Republican 'blood tax'.

Between 60,000 and 120,000 men fought under the sign of the sacred heart and the white cockade [**doc. 8**]. They covered all social groups, with a predominance of artisans and peasants. It was not, as has sometimes been assumed, simply a noble and peasant revolt, for textile artisans provided most of the initial zeal and local leadership at village level. Although non-juring priests did not take up arms, they were crucial in rallying support for the Vendéan 'armies' and organising supplies. Nobles were at the head of the larger armies **(93, ch. 13)**. The revolt continued to expand between March and June, partly because the Republican government attempted at first to put it down with undertrained and undisciplined troops: raw volunteers and amateurish detachments of the National Guard. Regular troops were required on the eastern frontier and to deal with revolts in Lyon and the south. On the face of it, Republican forces had little to beat, for the counter-revolutionary armies were scarcely armies at all. Unstable federations of local units, they were poorly organised, weakly disciplined and possessed only makeshift weapons and obsolete firearms. More of a home guard than an army, the rebels fought quick intense engagements and then went back home. They lacked either the will or the organisation to occupy and administer the towns they captured. If they met seasoned troops on a plain or defending a town, they were at a serious disadvantage. After midsummer, regular troops were sent to the west and succeeded in confining the rebellion to the four departments, thus beginning the long process of attrition which lasted until the flight of the rebels after late October, although the Vendée was to rise again in 1795, 1796, 1815 and 1832 **(120)**.

It took a long time to put down the rebellion because the artisans and peasants of the *bocage* introduced a form of guerrilla warfare into western Europe. They used the thick hedges, sunken roads and trees to snipe at Republican forces, then melt away into the friendly country-side. If the Republican government in Paris had not taken the Vendée sufficiently seriously at first, tending to dismiss it as a flash-in-the-pan Royalist and/or English plot, they soon realised the potential danger. The long and bitter struggle in the west radicalised the course of the Revolution and provided the chief justification for the Terror; it was in the west that the Terror claimed its largest number of victims and that the worst atrocities took place. Deputies in Paris were soon to see the Vendée as the major threat to the survival of France. Not only did it pin down an army needed on the eastern frontier, but the strips of Atlantic coast seized by the Vendéans were an open invitation for English and *émigré* armies to attempt a landing. Therefore the necessity of putting down the Vendée rebellion lay behind the creation of the various institutions of the Terror at both national and local level. The Vendée rising forced more and more Frenchmen into making a straight choice: for or against the Revolution, for the *tricoleur* or the white flag **(116, ch. 6)**.

Resistance to the Republican government was not confined to the Vendée. Rural revolts against conscription and in defence of the Church were widespread in the provinces. Whilst the alleged 'Royalist plot' did not exist in the Vendée, it certainly did in Brittany, where troops and National Guards were despatched to check it **(121)**. There were also a series of urban revolutions in what the Montagnards termed the 'Federalist revolt'. In Lyon and Marseille, Republicans were divided amongst themselves, so that moderates and counter-revolutionaries, having been expelled from municipal government in August 1792, were now able to take advantage of the crisis situation and return to the attack. Lyon, Marseille, Caen and Bordeaux were in the hands of Montagnards by the end of May. The revolt at Lyon, where the Jacobin mayor was captured and shot, was potentially lethal, for it gave the counter-revolution the chance to cut the Republic in two and hive off the eastern and frontier areas. In both Marseille and Caen, prosperous Girondin moderates gained considerable popular support for their seizure of power, since opposition to military conscription and the *représentants en mission* could, for many people, outweigh fear of invasion and dissatisfaction with high prices (122; 126; 131; 18, ch. 7). At the same time, there were sections of the common people who remained fired by Montagnard diatribes against *'les riches'*, so that the Federalist revolts were partly motivated by bourgeois fears for their property.

FALL OF THE GIRONDINS

As civil war became a reality in the summer of 1793, Royalists and Girondin moderates came together to defend order and property against a combination of *sans culottes* and Montagnards. Inside and outside the Convention the two groups became more closely linked to opposing social interests, as antagonism between rich and poor increased because of the economic crisis and *sans culotte* demands for forced loans on the rich to finance the war and subsidise controlled food prices. Pétion, the former radical mayor of Paris, now on the right, wrote in his *Lettre aux Parisiens:* 'Your property is threatened and you are shutting your eyes to the danger. It is war between the haves and the have-nots.'

While many Girondins still regarded the Revolution as over and desired only to consolidate the gains of the past, the Montagnards and their popular supporters urged strong government by a ruthless executive in the interests of social justice and, if necessary, at the expense of individual liberty. Charging some of the Girondins with being accomplices of the treacherous Dumouriez and others with being instigators of the Federalist plot, the Montagnards aimed to sieze power and impose their own revolutionary programme, although they wished to do so without becoming prisoners of the militant *sans culottes*. Through their newspapers and the network of clubs affiliated to the

Jacobins, the Montagnards and the Paris Commune publicised *sans culotte* demands for the expulsion of the Girondin deputies from the Convention. On 20 April the Commune declared itself 'in a state of insurrection' until food supplies for Paris were guaranteed. A great popular demonstration was held in the capital on 4 May for controlled food prices. The Convention responded by swallowing its liberal economic principles and decreeing the *Maximum* on the price of grain and flour. On 8 May Robespierre demanded the creation of an *armée révolutionnaire,* composed of *sans culottes,* to go out into the country-side and prise grain from the grasp of avaricious peasants and hoarding farmers who held on to stocks in the hope of further price increases.

While the Girondin deputies were slandered as traitors and counter-revolutionaries from press and platform, the Convention decreed the arrest of agitators like Varlet and Hébert and the appointment of a commission of twelve to search out plans for an insurrection. It suc-ceeded only in provoking the insurrection it was trying to prevent, for *sans culottes* invaded the Convention on 27 May, got the commission dissolved and the prisoners released. During the following two days the Paris sections assembled and 'fraternised', establishing a rather mysterious central revolutionary committee. The tocsin rang on the 31 May, while sectional leaders organized a revolutionary guard of 20,000 and put to the Convention a programme which included taxation of the rich to provide poor relief and subsidise food prices, a purge of nobles and 'moderates' in the army and civil administration, the creation of the *armée révolutionnaire* and the arrest of the commission of twelve, plus twenty-two Girondin deputies and two ministers. There then followed a brief lull, as the Montagnards debated whether to endorse so radical a programme, which would certainly not be welcomed in the provinces. Nor did they wish to see the *sans culottes* gain an absolute and bloody victory which would give them effective power; the *sans culotte* tail must not wag the Montagnard dog (71, ch. 8).

Nevertheless, the Montagnard leaders decided that they could break the Girondins in the Convention and still hold the *sans culottes* in check. On 2 June a force of 20,000 from the sections surrounded the Convention and, without the bloodshed of previous *journées,* procured the desired arrests. This was the third great revolution, following 14 July 1789 and 10 August 1792. Stalemate at the centre was now over. Property-owning and financial interests had been dealt another blow, as had representative parliamentary government. An extreme but fervent minority of Montagnards had taken control of the Convention and the nation. Such a victory can be seen as an aggressive bid for power (99, ch. 7), or as defensive action by the *sans culottes,* threatened by hunger, invasion and social reaction (**20,** part ii, ch. 2; **22,** book iv, ch. 2). There were elements of both. The question now was whether the Jacobins could defeat the foreign enemy, put down counter-revolution and retain the support of the *sans culottes*. The latter assumed that a purge of the Convention would lead to the immediate implementation of their own social and economic demands.

THE DESPOTISM OF LIBERTY

In fact the *sans culottes* got little immediate satisfaction: no *armée révolutionnaire,* no purges of the army and administration, no wave of arrests of suspects, no distribution of arms among themselves. Montagnards were reluctant to be linked too closely to the militant *sans culottes,* as the Paris sections were still divided between militants and moderates and Roux's *enragé* programme met strong opposition from the provinces (**104,** i, ch. 1). Moreover, the Montagnards and the Committee of Public Safety were inclined to pursue a policy of moderation in order to justify the overthrow of the Girondins on 31 May, a *journée* which was condemned by the assemblies of seventy-six departments. Federalist revolts stemmed not only from the desire of prosperous men in the provinces to maintain their political authority and social position, but also from resentment at the domination of the Revolution by Paris and direct action by popular militants against the legally-established Convention (**122; 130,** ch. 2). This moderate policy paid initial dividends. The Federalists were unable to focus discontent on a ruthless popular dictatorship and, although they posed a critical threat to the Republic, the movement did not spread very much. The fact that the Federalists were badly led and lacked any central coherent political programme provided the Republic with some small comfort in a situation where at least a quarter of the country was in counter-revolutionary hands.

Albeit unwilling to accept the *enragé* recipe of violence, intimidation and strict economic controls, the Montagnards were nevertheless obliged to implement some popular measures: the speeding up of the work of the Revolutionary tribunal, the resumption of the sale of *émigré* property, the division and distribution of common land in villages which demanded it, and the complete abolition of remaining feudal rights. But non-feudal contracts were to be honoured; in other words property rights in general were upheld. A further step in the search for national unity was the new Constitution of 1793, demanded by both Girondins and Jacobins. It included the principles of universal suffrage, liberty of the press and the right of insurrection 'when the government violates the rights of the people'. But property rights were emphasised, the Convention choosing to ignore Robespierre's schemes for the limitation of property. On the other hand, the Republic accepted its responsibility for providing a basic subsistence standard of living, public assistance for the unemployed and infirm, and universal primary education. However, the Constitution of 1793 was very much a political manoeuvre and was never put into practice. Frequent elections would have meant prolonged political turmoil, while constant referenda would have crippled the executive. Many voted for it only because they hoped it would mean the end of both the Convention and the war. Not surprisingly, therefore, the Constitution was kept under an arch of cedarwood and virtually forgotten (**124**, ch. 2; **17** ch. 9).

Although the Jacobins saw to it that Jacques Roux was expelled from his section and the Cordeliers Club when he bitterly criticised their policy of conciliation, the Convention and the Committee of Public Safety were pushed inexorably away from moderation by the exigencies of war and rebellion (**114, 115**). Early in July the Vendéan rebels destroyed a Republican army and almost seized the great port of Nantes. On the frontiers, in July and August, Mainz fell to the Prussians, the Austrians invaded north-eastern France, the Spaniards crossed the Pyrenees and threatened Bayonne and Perpignan, the Sardinians marched across the south-eastern frontier, and in October Alsace was invaded. With the Republic on the brink of defeat, Danton made overtures for peace. What would be the fate of a defeated France was grimly forecast by the action of the Allies in shooting and hanging all those in the invaded northern region who had played any active part in the Revolution. Not only was a massive military effort required on the frontiers, but major campaigns had also to be mounted against the Vendée, Lyon, Marseille and Toulon. Although Marseille was taken by Republican troops on 25 August, the royalists of Toulon handed the premier French naval base over to the English fleet two days later, whilst the bloody seige of Lyon lasted until early October. In Paris, the murder of Marat, the idol of the *sans culottes,* on 13 July was rumoured to be a result of a Norman royalist plot. France, it seemed, was riddled with traitors (**22**, book iv, ch. 2).

Such an atmosphere of military defeat, counter-revolution and treason intensified popular pressure for ruthless action against external enemies, internal rebels, and those men responsible for local government in the provinces who seemed willing to resist Paris and the popular movement and very reluctant to defend France against the foreign armies to the last drop of their blood. Only a new alliance between the Montagnard leaders and the militant *sans culottes* appeared likely to save France from anarchy and collapse; only the *sans culottes* existed as a sufficiently powerful revolutionary force to sustain the government in crushing 'aristocrats, egoists and moderates' by means of organized intimidation on a grand scale. This line of reasoning among Jacobins in the Convention and government was encouraged by a hardening of opinion among the militant *sans culottes* themselves **(150)**. After a prolonged struggle in the Paris sections, the moderates were overcome and increased support gained in the clubs and popular societies for a programme which included widespread arrests of suspects, speedier justice, the trial of the queen and the Girondin deputies under house arrest, a mass conscription of the population for the army and the war effort and the creation of an *armée révolutionnaire* **(104**, i, ch. 1) **[doc. 14]**.

Besides the desire for repression, there was also a renewed demand for strict economic regulation. The decree of 26 July threatening food hoarders with death had done little to solve the mounting food crisis, the high price of bread and the downward spiral of the *assignat* **(71**, ch. 8). Such a situation could easily result in another popular *journée* and the government took swift action to head it off. Commissioners were appointed to deal with the question of food supply, whilst *représentants en mission* were encouraged to requisition provincial grain for the Paris markets **(134)**. A forced loan on the rich was to act as an indirect food subsidy. However, none of these measures proved very effective, bitterly resented though they were by Federalists and moderates in the provinces. Much more dramatic and important was the decreeing of the *levée en masse* on 23 August, a measure which has also been demanded by the *menu peuple* **[doc. 9]**. All French men and women between eighteen and sixty were liable to be called up for war work. Bachelors and widowers without children between eighteen and twenty-five formed the 'first requisition' for the army. Recruitment on such a scale implied not only a new conception of total war, but also some degree of firm government control over industry and the economy. Ironically, conscription helped to deepen the famine crisis, which was to last three years, by depriving the countryside of healthy manpower and creating a chronic shortage of agricultural labour **(106**, ch. 3).

As stocks of food in the capital continued to fall, so popular demands for general price control increased. Women, always keen advocates of price fixation, were bitter at having to queue for seven hours for unpalatable bread **(117)**. On 4 and 5 September, encouraged by the Paris Commune, there were serious *sans culotte* demonstrations in Paris for higher wages and a better supply of bread. After temporarily pacifying the crowd with slogans like 'death to aristocrats and hoarders!', the Convention was forced to make concessions. Needy *sans culottes* were to be paid for attending revolutionary committees and sectional assemblies, although the latter were restricted to two meetings per week (102, ch. 5). A Parisian *armée révolutionaire* of 60,000 was created, mainly composed of *sans culottes,* to act as an instrument of Terror by ensuring food supplies for the capital and by assisting the regular army and volunteer forces against Lyon and the Vendée (104, i, ch. 1). Yet the immediate problem of food shortage and high prices remained; the Convention, against its will, had to bow before popular pressure and on 11 September decreed a new maximum on grain and flour, and on 29 September a General Maximum which fixed prices for soap, salt and tobacco and stipulated that the localities fix the price of other basic consumer goods at a level one-third above the prices of 1790. To the surprise of the *sans culottes,* wages were also fixed, at 50 per cent above 1790 levels; something which, needless to say, the *sans culottes* had *not* demanded. This ambitious attempt to control prices and wages demanded a considerable administrative machinery, headed by the Food Commission. (72, ch. 7; 124, ch. 2; 18, ch. 8; 160; 71, ch. 8).

Such measures cemented the alliance between the Jacobins and the popular movement and provided an essential foundation for the Revolutionary government which emerged in the autumn of 1793 — the beginning of the Year II. Terror was now 'the order of the day'. A new law of suspects on 17 September cast the net wide to include 'those who, by their conduct or associations, by their words or writing, are monstrous partisans of tyranny and federalism and are enemies of liberty' [doc. 13]. Terror in the provinces was paralleled by the trial and guillotining of Marie Antoinette, Madame Roland and the Girondin deputies in October. A massive Jacobin propaganda campaign was launched throughout the country to rally support for the Revolutionary government against its enemies (89, ch. 7). The determination of the government was displayed in the ferocious intensity of the Republican attack on the rebels at Lyon, which fell on 9 October. Declaring that 'Lyon no longer exists', the Committee of Public Safety ordered the destruction of the houses of the rich in the city, henceforth named Ville-affranchie, and commenced savage reprisals which led to the shooting of nearly 2,000 rebels. (132; 125, ch. 7) [doc. 16].

The Vendéans in the west were defeated soon afterwards. On 10 October the constitution was formally suspended and the government declared revolutionary until the peace, while the Committee of Public Safety consolidated its position as the head of the executive (151). Those who had done nothing for the Revolution were to be regarded as against it; no quarter was to be given to counter-revolutionaries [doc. 19]. As Saint-Just put it, with characteristic brutality, in the Convention: 'The indifferent must be punished as well as traitors; you must punish the passive ones in the Republic . . . we must govern with iron those who cannot be ruled by justice'.

7 Robespierre and the Reign of Virtue

THE ORGANISATION OF TERROR

The consolidation of the Revolutionary government on 10 October led to a new spirit of vigorous administration. What was, in effect, a dictatorial régime composed of a resolute minority of Jacobins and *sans culottes*, imposed its will on the mass of the population in the name of the 'supreme law of public safety'. In the crisis of war and rebellion, the principle of decentralised government which had been accepted in 1789 was now reversed. New institutions were created alongside the departmental, district and municipal authorities with the aim of subordinating the provinces to centralised rule from Paris, rule which was transmitted to the localities by means of *représentants en mission* and various *commissaires.*

At the head of the Revolutionary government stood the Convention, the symbol of national unity, but in fact increasingly unrepresentative of the nation as a whole. Although the Convention did a great deal of work, handling masses of petitions and addresses and scrutinising the reports of the committees, real executive authority rested in the hands of the Committee of Public Safety, the twelve members of which governed France in the Year II, having come together on the Committee between July and September. Each of them originated in the petty bourgeoisie of the *ancien régime,* but they were of divergent social outlook and political opinions. If Billaud-Varenne and Collot d'Herbois inclined to radical *sans culotte* opinions, then Lindet and Carnot were social conservatives. All four, however, as well as the other members of the Committee, were willing to sink such differences in the service of *La Patrie.* The C.P.S. worked tremendously hard: at the committee rooms in the Tuileries from 7 a.m. to noon, in the Convention during the afternoon, meeting again at 8 p.m. and working until the small hours before going to their camp beds. In fact all twelve never got round the green table at the same time, for there was a degree of specialisation in the Committee and some members were usually away on missions to the provinces; only Robespierre and Barère never left Paris. Decisions were taken in common and required at least three signatures; there was no chairman and discussions were secret. Until Thermidor, the C.P.S.

was unanimous in its collective opinion as far as the public was concerned. It was a committee of the Convention, who confirmed its powers monthly and where its decisions were discussed, usually being defended by Barère, Couthon and Robespierre. (**128; 127**, ch. 2).

The C.P.S. controlled other committees, ministers and commissions, at the same time delegating its powers to the *représentants en mission.* These constituted the most important single element in the structure of the provincial Terror and accounted for over a third of the members of the Convention during the winter of 1793-94, being attached to the departments and the army. Their orders were regarded as decrees of the Convention, for each *représentant* was held to be a personification of national sovereignty. A minority of them, for example Carrier at Nantes and Fouché at Lyon, were powerful proconsuls who ruthlessly shaped policy in their areas and had considerable freedom of manoeuvre, although they were supposed to report to the C.P.S. every ten days. The *représentants* were the chief agents in linking the departments to the Convention and the C.P.S. and in trying to force local authorities to implement the decisions of the central government. A France brought to the verge of disintegration by the Federalist revolt was to be forced into acceptance of administrative uniformity so that resources could be coordinated for the war effort. To resist a *représentant* was to resist the sovereign will of the people.

In fact the system of *représentants* did not work as intended, at least not before early 1794, and their activities contributed to the fact that the Terror was initially anarchic. They were sometimes in rivalry with each other; the same department could often be allotted to more than one of them; they frequently followed their own differing temperaments and opinions when establishing local terrorist institutions and repressing federalism and royalism. Javogues, the *représentant* in the department of the Loire, was at odds with both the government and his colleagues. Not only did he fail to report regularly to the C.P.S., but he also consistently ignored instructions from Paris, keeping in being the departmental *armée révolutionnaire* after the Convention had abolished it and carrying through an intense programme of dechristianisation in defiance of the wishes of the central government. Insubordinate ultra revolutionary *représentants* like Javogues made the Terror anarchic in that, by pursuing individualist policies, they prevented their departments from participating in a coordinated national system and weakened the concept of a centralized Terror (**130**, chs 3,10,12). Moreover, slow communications between the C.P.S. and the *représentants* put a brake on the development of a smooth, uniform system; messages from Paris took eight to twelve days to reach Marseille and a fortnight to reach the Ariège.

Besides the *représentants*, there was also a multitude of *commissaires*, acting as agents of various bodies: the C.P.S., the Committee of General Security, the *représentants* themselves, the food commission and various special repressive missions to the provinces. Below them was a further layer of *sous-commissaires*. Although these commissioners could sometimes cause confusion, they were an essential element of the repressive and administrative aspects of the Terror, forming a direct link between local populations and higher authorities. Having considerable power at a local level, they were instrumental, like the *armées révolutionnaires*, in taking the Terror to the villages **(138)**. The Committee of General Security formed another major branch of the Terror. Composed, like the C.P.S., of twelve men, it was in practice a ministry of Revolutionary police, preparing dossiers and inquiries, interviewing witnesses and despatching agents throughout France concerned with counter espionage and rooting out *incivisme*. It too was a committee of the Convention, but was subordinated to the C.P.S., with whom it developed a certain rivalry **(158)**.

Apart from the *représentants*, the primary instrument of the Terror in the departments until the end of 1793, and in the Paris region until March 1794, was the *armées révolutionnaires*, the activities of which have been so deeply studied by Professor Cobb **(104)**. Their task was to be agents of the civil power, to maintain links between the civil authorities and the armed forces, to ensure the requisitioning of towns by prising food from the hands of the peasants and to spread the Revolution in the countryside [**doc. 17**]. As apostles of Revolutionary orthodoxy, the *armées* aimed to strike fear in both counter-revolutionaries and the merely indifferent and to act as an instrument of vengeance and vigilance, working with local popular societies and revolutionary committees. It was the *armées* which took a leading role in encouraging patriotic *fêtes*, in using the new Revolutionary calendar, in founding 'schools of liberty' for the uneducated, and in attacking religion in the name of the trinity of Revolution, Republic and Democracy. Above all, they were involved in assisting regular troops in assaults on the major counter-revolutionary centres, besides enforcing the *maximum* and trying to ensure the supply of grain and other basic commodities to urban markets. A practical manifestation of *sans culotte* attitudes and priorities, the *armées révolutionnaires* were very much concerned with the interests of the small consumer against the richer classes, and with the economic interests of the towns against those of the countryside. Hoarders were regarded as the worst sort of counter-revolutionary **(104**, vol. i, introduction, ch. 1).

The *armées révolutionnaires* must not be confused with the regular troops or volunteers for the army. Although they were under the authority of the military commanders in the war zones and under the nominal control of the districts and municipalities in other areas, they possessed a good deal of independence. Composed of citizens whose Revolutionary orthodoxy was assured by the granting of *certificats de civisme* and who were not subject to military discipline, the *armées* regarded themselves as citizens rather than soldiers. Officers were elected by the ranks and discipline was always difficult to enforce, especially when a detachment could amount to no more than half-a-dozen dirty, swearing, shouting *sans culottes*. The origins of members of the *armées* were diverse. The headquarters of the 6,000 strong Parisian army contained many bright young men whose revolutionary principles were questionable; many of the officers were ex-N.C.O.s in the regular army or had been *gendarmes* or members of the National Guard; many of the ranks were composed of the shopkeepers and artisans of Parisian *sans culotterie,* with their hatred of luxury, idleness, hoarders and religion, and their fondness for food and wine and pleasure in iconoclasm and destruction. Motives for joining were similarly varied: sheer patriotism, high pay, the necessity to flee creditors or pregnant girls. The departmental armies, amounting to about 40,000 men operating in sixty-six departments, had similar tasks to that of Paris. There were also some small 'unofficial' *armées* which emerged during administrative confusion and anarchy. Some of them were little more than groups of bandits and gangsters clinging to the wheels of the Revolutionary wagon (**104**, vol. ii, chs 3, 4).

If the *armées révolutionnaires* were a product of administrative anarchy, they themselves did much to deepen it. Their areas of operation frequently overlapped and conflicted and there was very little really firm control over their activities. Sometimes they were guided by the *représentant en mission,* sometimes by civil commissioners, local popular societies and revolutionary committees. A few of them, for example in the Loire, remained firmly under the control of the old districts and municipalities (**130**, ch. 6). Just how effective the *armées* were is not easy to assess. Sneered at as 'butter and cheese soldiers', most of their members were fairly old, between thirty-five and fifty, unfit and ill-disciplined. The departmental armies, unlike that of Paris, also included some of the very poor and foreigners, who had more interest in pay than in Revolutionary principles. Despite cases of indiscipline and pillage, especially of food and drink, they were not on the whole either criminal or excessively brutal, although in certain circumstances they could be hard and cruel [**doc.15**]. The most extreme example, the *armée Marat* at Nantes, could at least claim the justification of being almost swamped in a sea of counter-revolution and having seen the bodies of their comrades savagely mutilated by the Chouans (**104**, i, ch. 5; **125**, part ii, ch. 8; **127**, ch. 9).

The *armées* never managed to enforce the *maximum* completely; but did largely succeed in ensuring supplies of bread and grain for Paris, though they had less success with butter, eggs and meat [doc.17]. They also had a good record on the collection of church bells and gold and silver plate for the war effort. These achievements were in spite of the absence of any real regional economic policy. Again, they were the chief agents in the rather unsystematic dechristianisation campaign, though here too they alienated the countryside, particularly its women. Certainly the Republican soldier was fed and clothed in the Year II, and victory at Fleurus owed a good deal to the efforts of the *armées revolutionnaires*. Repressive missions, the most important being that of the Parisian *armée* to Lyon, and the masses of arrests undertaken by the *armées* were less useful, in that they were costly and impossible to mount without regular troops, as well as intensifying royalism, pushing many into counter-revolution and creating friction with local authorities (**104**, part ii, chs 1-4)[doc.16].

The Revolutionary government had supported the creation of the *armées* in the autumn of 1793 with considerable reluctance, fore-seeing problems of control and coordination of their operations. Essentially forced on the government by *sans culotte* opinion, the *armées* did not last long. Those in the departments were abolished by the law of 14 Frimaire (6 December 1793), the Parisian *armée* lasting until 7 Germinal (27 March 1794). For the central government turned on the *armées* as part of its policy of putting a brake on the anarchic Terror and the dechristianisation campaign and enforcing the authority of the C.P.S. and C.G.S. against local initiative and 'indiscipline', which, it alleged, led to 'federalism'. The Parisian *armée* in particular seemed to threaten its authority and become a tool of the Hébertists and 'military plotters' (**104**, part ii, ch. 7).

At a local level, an essential part of the structure of the Terror was formed by the revolutionary committees *(comités révolutionnaires)* decreed to exist in every commune from 21 March 1793, although many had come into existence after 10 August 1792. Each committee had twelve elected members and assisted the 'constituted authorities' − the districts and municipalities − in executing Revolutionary measures, often at a mundane level: issuing *certificats de civisme* and arrest warrants, visiting prisons, destroying such signs of 'feudalism' as the *fleur-de-lys* on public buildings, and generally enforcing Revolutionary orthodoxy. These revolutionary committees were the cornerstone of the edifice of repression, having been mobilised against federalism and the consequent breakdown of the local government system [doc.25]. Usually their members were composed of the active minority of the revolutionary clubs in urban areas; as with other agencies of the Terror, their members were both more lethargic and thinner on the ground in rural districts (124, ch. 3; 130, ch. 5).

Equally essential to the operation of Revolutionary justice, itself an expression of the 'vengeance of the people' and the determination of the government, were the Revolutionary tribunals. That of Paris was rapidly expanded after September 1793, condemning 177 out of 395 accused before 30 December. Those in the departments, however, were often dilatory, being composed of painstaking lawyers of the *ancien régime*; that at Metz executed nobody before the end of November. To speed up Revolutionary justice, extraordinary tribunals were set up without juries in various counter-revolutionary localities, such as Brest, Nancy, Lyon, Marseille, Nimes and Toulon (127, ch. 9; 131, ch. 8) [docs 19, 20, 21].

Here, too, there was an anarchy similar to that of the operations of the *armées révolutionnaires*, for there also existed military commissions and army tribunals pronouncing swift death sentences. After 14 Frimaire priority was reserved for the Paris tribunal, but others survived and were reinvigorated in the spring of 1794. Justice dispensed by the Revolutionary tribunals was speedy, without right of appeal. Javogues, the ultrarevolutionary *représentant* in the Loire, felt that twenty-four hours between the arrival and burial of a suspect was ample time, although it is significant that the tribunal in the Loire was one of the most slow-moving and pettifogging (130, ch. 9).

Much of the impetus behind the Terror stemmed from economic motives: the desire of the government to mobilise productive resources to feed the urban population and supply the armies. After December 1793 the C.P.S. had considerable success, but in the period of the anarchic Terror there was no really soundly based economic programme. The massive efforts of the Food Committee *(Commission des Subsistances)* to encourage new agricultural techniques brought only limited results; requisitioning tended to be piecemeal, as some areas were stripped of their stocks of food and had themselves to undertake requisitions against weaker neighbours, whilst other areas were hardly touched (134). There was no general rationing system; hoarding and black markets continued to flourish. Farmers, upset by the *maximum* and by the attacks of the *armées révolutionnaires*, tended to hold onto their stocks of food at a time of such political uncertainty. Local taxes on the rich did little to mitigate a growing budget deficit, although the situation improved with a forced loan graduated on income, which was combined with the consolidation of the national debt. Certainly there was no serious attempt to transform the basic economic structure of society.

So far as the war effort was concerned, the Revolutionary government had a striking record, for its policies involved a new conception of warfare. A politicised and revolutionary army was created, which had faith in the cause of the Republic against its enemies. The *levée en masse* raised a nation in arms against foreign rulers and imbued it with a desire to liberate and 'educate' subject peoples. Military service became the ultimate expression of patriotic enthusiasm, as well as providing a convenient ladder of social mobility. A new, mobile citizen army gave opportunities to young officers unthinkable in the armies of the *ancien régime* and, despite insubordination and desertion, proved a formidable fighting force by the spring of 1794 (**124**, ch. 4; **22**, book iv, ch. 2). To supply the new army, France became something of a vast military workshop, organised by Carnot and the commissioners of war, who put out contracts, fixed wages, enforced industrial discipline and brought the knowledge of scientists to bear on war production. Popular enthusiasm for the war effort was exemplified by the campaign to extract saltpetre for gunpowder: over 6,000 workshops were opened and a ninefold increase in production achieved (**127**, chs 6-10) [**doc.25**].

TERRORISTS AND COUNTER-TERRORISTS

Members of the institutions of the Terror were an extremely varied group of men and by no means all of them were militants. Generally speaking, they were townsmen from lowland areas. Rural districts, and towns in mountainous and woody country, tended to be either counter-revolutionary or indifferent. The Terror was very much an urban phenomenon. Such townsmen as formed cogs in the machinery of the Terror followed a variety of occupations and formed no cohesive social group. This is true even of the Paris *sans culottes*. Here, as in the provinces, those involved in terrorist institutions did not include the very poor and the 'floating population', although the latter provided large numbers of recruits for the army (**177**). In the Year II, 26.2 per cent of members of Paris civil committees lived off private incomes, whilst over 60 per cent of the more popularly recruited revolutionary committees were skilled craftsmen or shopkeepers. Provincial terrorists were more often than not men of some financial resources. Occupying a post cost money, except in the regularly paid *armées révolutionnaires,* and salaries were always well in arrears. Popular societies and clubs usually stipulated entrance fees and demanded both literacy and a considerable amount of a member's time. Certainly in the Loire, as Dr Lucas shows, terrorists cannot be equated with the Paris *sans culottes,* for the *menu peuple* were almost entirely excluded (**130**, ch. 11). Neither were they the upper-crust of local society. What the Terror tended to do in many areas was to bring to the fore men who had already participated in public life, but not at a very high level. Now they had a chance to eject old ruling groups and dominate the localities. Personal feuds and family antagonisms were not the least of the motives of the terrorists at a local level; nor was the desire for office and employment. The Terror gave to many frustrated men a heady taste for power and access to occupations which had previously been denied them. Often this meant, not so much a rise from obscurity, as a transfer of power from the upper to the lower echelons of the old society of the *ancien régime.*

Whatever their social situation, however, militant terrorists were democrats who distrusted great wealth. Yet such distrust was not based on class antagonism. There were rich cotton manufacturers and wealthy property owners, as well as artisans, in the revolutionary societies of Lille; many moderates or counter-revolutionaries came from the same social group, or even families, as the terrorists (**133**; **130**, ch. 11). Militant terrorism was more an individual than a class characteristic. Most of the terrorists were not very young, often between thirty-five and forty, and included both violent, unstable men and amiable *bon bougres* with little taste for large-scale repression. The factors which inclined men to become terrorists varied to the point of incalculability. Similar urban areas, in close proximity, could show significant variations in the intensity of the Terror. Some became terrorists for reasons of self-defence in areas of counter-revolutionary or federalist revolt; others were motivated by ties of blood, marriage, friendship, business relationships and neighbourhood. Above all, however, there was the motive of political beliefs. How a man reacted to events like the fall and execution of the king, the September Massacres, the economic crisis and military defeat tended to be the major determinant of which side he joined. Such reactions would often to some extent be predetermined by his attitude on the religious issue of 1790-91.

Yet political reactions and attitudes often accompanied lesser motives: the chance to escape from a drab existence played its part in the careers of men like Javogues, Carrier and Carnot; the chance to get his own back on rich timber merchants played a part in the motivation of Nicholas Guenot, although his rise from rural obscurity and viciousness to becoming an agent of the C.G.S. was assisted by his criminal contacts and extremely violent temperament (130). Other terrorists were former priests or dull and obscure provincial lawyers who constantly trimmed their sails to the prevailing political wind, or were minor officials who took their chance of quick profits from government confiscations and contracts (140; 129, ch. 3).

The sources of counter-terrorism were equally varied; indeed, the choice of Terror or counter-revolution was sometimes almost accidental. The counter-terror was essentially local and individual, for it lacked any national programme and drew its strength from habit and tradition, especially in the south. There were many men who were simply apathetic, although the Republic classed the indifferent as counter-revolutionary [doc.22]. They were often able to ignore the Terror and live outside it, for the government of the Year II lacked the resources of a Stalin or Hitler, having, in Cobb's phrase, 'to rely on a man on a horse'. Such people often lived in mountains, woods or other inaccessible areas; some were brigands and bandits who carried on with their daily task of robbery and grisly murder. Nor were the very poor much involved in the Terror, except in so far as they were the victims of it (177). Many people, especially in the south, were counter-revolutionary because of local pride and resentment of Paris and its high-flown Revolutionary phrases (129, introduction, ch. 1). Women were frequently hostile because of the damage done by the Revolution to the family, the Church and the shopping basket (117).

THE EFFECTS OF THE TERROR

The most striking effect of the Terror was the increase in government repression. Before 1789 governments were anything but genteel and people were used to seeing criminals branded, tortured and broken on the wheel. Since its beginning the Revolution had been shaped by violence, but such violence tended to come from crowds rather than the Revolutionary régime. What was new after September 1793 was that Terror was organised and became for the first time a deliberate policy of government (127, ch. 2). It may well be that, had this government repression not existed, more people would have been killed in popular outbursts of violence, for below the elegant surface of society at the top, the French people were brutal and bloodthirsty. Yet there were no popular bloody *journées* during the Year II.

Before the fall of the Robespierrists in Thermidor (July 1794), something like 30,000 people had been killed by the official Terror. Such a number is small by twentieth-century standards, but it horrified European opinion at the time. Rather than the nobles of legend, the majority of victims were ordinary men and women from the lower ranks of society (**126**, chs. 2, 5). About 10,000 died in stinking, over-crowded gaols. The most barbarous aspect of the Terror was repression against counter-revolutionaries after Republican victories in the civil war. At Lyon, Fouché and Collot d'Herbois had hundreds of suspects shot by cannon-fire and blasted into open graves [**doc.16**]. At Nantes, Carrier condoned the *noyades,* when over 2,000 prisoners were pushed from rafts into the icy waters of the Loire (**127**, chs 7, 9). Such extreme atrocities took place in strong counter-revolutionary areas, where royalists, Vendéans and Chouans had themselves killed Republicans by barbarous methods. Over 70 per cent of executions under the Terror took place in limited areas of the west and south-east; thus Paris was swamped by the provinces as far as the number of victims was concerned. In fact the region around Paris, plus the central areas of France, suffered least. About half of France was scarcely affected by the repressive Terror: six departments had no executions at all and thirty-seven had less than ten each. Only the war zones on the frontiers and the vulnerable coasts could rival the areas of civil war in the intensity of the Terror (**126**, ch. 3).

The largest number of executions under the Terror took place during the period of the 'anarchic' Terror between October 1793 and January 1794. Yet such intensity of repression was qualified by geographical variations even in areas of repression, for there could be towns and villages in such areas hardly touched by the Terror. Indeed, some places were hardly touched by the French Revolution at all, let alone the Terror. The village of Authieux, near Rouen, had 289 inhabitants in 1789. Its register of municipal deliberations makes no mention of 14 July 1789, 10 August 1792 or 9 Thermidor 1794, whilst the inefficiency of the new administrative personnel in the Year II reveals the inadequacy of the attempt of the Revolutionary government at administrative centralization. 'No political event between 1789 and 1793', writes Professor Soboul, 'troubled the quiet life of the parish, sheltered from the general movement which transformed the nation' (**136**). The only approach to anything like Revolutionary crisis in Authieux was resentment at the requisitioning of grain to feed nearby Rouen.

It is far from easy to summarise the effects of the Terror on the population as a whole. There were those who paid with their lives; there were those who were unaffected; men from the same area and social group could find either opportunity or disaster during the Year II.

A more meaningful approach is to ask how the Terror affected a particular region (130; 131; 177). Nevertheless, some attempt can be made at generalisation. It is doubtful whether Revolution and Terror did much for the very poor, a fifth of the population of France in 1790. Local militants on revolutionary committees tended to be anxious to protect property and preserve public order, as well as possessing a mean attitude to charity, based on a concept of the 'deserving' (that is, 'revolutionary') poor. Poor women, runaway and delinquent children were hounded mercilessly by agents of the Revolutionary government. Adequate treatment of the poor was one of the most conspicuous failures of the Revolutionary government. Hospitals, schools and charitable institutions were hard hit by Revolutionary legislation. The abolition of the religious orders robbed them of staff; the abolition of feudal dues and rents took away their income. War brought disproportionate suffering to the poor, for they bore the main burden of disrupted trade, military recruitment and grain requisitions (178). Revolutionary decrees on poverty were nullified by a clumsily bureaucratic administrative apparatus, by ignorance of local circumstances and practice and, above all, by the fact that inflation, war and blockade absorbed the money needed to implement a centralized and state-controlled system of welfare. In large towns like Marseille, Bordeaux and Lyon, the problem of the urban poor was particularly acute and clearly deteriorated after 1789.

A Revolution so keen on the rights of man hardly gave a thought to those of woman. Total war, implying large armies and movement of workers into war industries meant a good deal of mobility and increased sexual opportunities for men. Married women were increasingly deserted: so were pregnant single girls. Many of them joined the ranks of prostitution, itself not the least of the expanding war industries. Such changes threatened the stability of the family at a time when dearth and high prices meant long queues for scarcely edible food and impossible strain on the family budgets of working women in the towns [doc.22]. Meanwhile a crisis in trade and the collapse of the luxury industries undermined women's employment. The woman who had proudly urged her sons to join the army, who spouted Revolutionary slogans, who poured out venom against priests and *émigrés,* became soured by economic deprivation and desperate attempts to feed her family. In the end she became, in the expressive words of Olwen Hufton, 'ultimately the worn-out, disillusioned, starving hag who sank to her knees in Year III to demand pardon of an offended Christ' (117).

Certainly the Terror gave opportunities to men for upward social mobility; in some areas the Terror seems almost to have been operated solely by former wig-makers (133). Such men were normally town-dwellers. If the Terror originated in the towns, then it created a good deal of antagonism in the countryside. There was no love lost between the *sans culottes* and the rural classes (106, book iii, part 2). Although many peasants profited from inflation and labour shortages, most of them disliked the manner in which townsmen operated the Terror to their own advantage: to feed themselves, to monopolise official posts and to get their hands on the confiscated wealth of the Church and *émigrés*. The urban classes, on the other hand, accused 'grasping peasants' of deliberately attempting to starve the towns and obstruct the operation of the Terror, thereby encouraging the enemies of the Republic.

Custom and habit carried such weight in the countryside that the Revolution was unable to change attitudes overnight. Religion remained powerful in rural France, especially among women; this was one reason for the antifeminism of the popular movement. Attacks by terrorists on priests and *fanatisme* did much to alienate people from the Revolution. Urban *sans culottes* developed cults of Marat, Lepeletier and Chalier, the Revolutionary martyrs, which involved a secularised political version of Catholic liturgy and imagery, but they remained largely confined to a minority of urban militants and helped to deepen hostility to the Revolution in much of the countryside (143) [doc. 14]. Nor did the succeeding cults of Reason and the Supreme Being do much to mitigate the effects of Revolutionary assaults on the Church, for the iconoclasm and violence of the dechristianisation campaign in the winter of 1793-94 sowed divisions in the country rather than contributed to national unity (141). A few village artisans may have welcomed the Terror, but the majority of peasants were glad to see the fall of Robespierre in Thermidor and the end of the despotism of liberty in late 1794. For the Terror chiefly benefited townsmen at all levels save the lowest. It was they who got access to jobs, to promotion in the army, to purchases of ecclesiastical and *émigré* property, to profits from war contracts, whilst the burden of war and mobilization fell most heavily on farmers and peasants.

SAINT MAXIMILIEN

The period of the 'Great Terror' from January to July 1794 is most closely associated with the name of Robespierre, the most prominent and widely known member of the Committee of Public Safety. Robespierre has always been at the very centre of historical contro-versy on the French Revolution; so much so that there are very few memorials to him in Republican France and no 'Rue Robespierre' in

Paris. Historians of the Right, as well as the Aulard school of liberal partisans of Danton, see him as an austere tyrant, whose personal ascendancy in late 1793 and early 1794 proved the antithesis of democracy and brought the Revolution to ruin and collapse in an orgy of executions. J.L. Talmon traces a remorselessly direct (and not very historical) line from the political philosophy of Rousseau, through the ideas and policies of Robespierre, to the modern totalitarian democracies of Lenin, Stalin and Hitler. What he calls Robespierre's 'democratic perfectionism' was 'inverted totalitarianism', since it was 'based on a fanatical belief that there could be no more than one legitimate popular will. The other wills stood condemned *a priori* as partial, selfish and illegitimate' (167, part ii, ch. 3). Robespierre has been accused of dictatorship, of desiring to create a personal cult, of employing the Grand Terror solely and cynically for the purpose of perpetuating himself in power (171).

Generally reviled in the nineteenth century, except by socialists like Buonarotti and Louis Blanc, Robespierre's reputation was rehabilitated by Albert Mathiez, for whom, as for so many Jacobins and *sans culottes* in 1792 and 1793, he was 'this saint of democracy'. Mathiez saw the Incorruptible as 'in no way a demagogue. He loved the people too much to flatter them . . . he was the schoolmaster of democracy . . . the incarnation of Revolutionary France in its most noble, most generous and most sincere aspects' (147, chs 1, 3; 23, book ii, ch. 2). Since Mathiez, historians have been divided on their assessment of Robespierre; so have French politicians. The bicentenary of his birth in 1958 provoked a good deal of acrimony in the municipal council of the city of Paris (172, foreword). Marxist historians are similarly divided; some see him as pointing the way to socialism (160), others are unable to forgive him for attacking the *enragés* and Hébertists and accuse him of betraying the interests of the common people in 1794 (150; 151).

It is true that to some extent Robespierre was the creature of circumstances, for whom Terror and the 'despotism of liberty' was a necessary response to war, treachery, internal rebellion and the danger of a 'military plot' (147, ch. 3). But there was more to it than that. Robespierre had a vision, whereby the Revolutionary government of the Year II aimed at perpetuating the existence of democratic rule and the life of the French Republic [doc. 23]. This vision was one shared by many Jacobins, particularly Saint-Just (127, ch. 11;154; 173, ch. 11). France would become, not merely a democratic Republic, but a republic of virtue. The end justified the means; to bring about such a glorious future justified the Terror. In his most memorable speech, delivered before the Convention on 5 February 1794 (17 Pluviôse), Robespierre exclaimed: 'If the aim of popular government in peacetime is virtue, then the aim of popular government in a time of Revolution is virtue and terror at one and the same time: virtue without which terror is disastrous, terror without which virtue is impotent' [doc. 24].

It is difficult to view Robespierre as other than a tragic figure, for his attempt to blend together Rousseauist political philosophy with the practical leadership of the Revolutionary government ended in failure and death. He was very much a man of the eighteenth-century Enlightenment, convinced of the supremacy of spiritual values and the eternal laws of reason. Only the application of fundamental moral principles in government could provide the antidote for political corruption and bring social happiness. Robespierre, in other words, saw politics as a branch of ethics. His basic political ideas were taken from Rousseau's *Social Contract,* as indeed were those of many Jacobins and *sans culottes,* though in a more indirect and unsystematic manner (152; 153). Like Rousseau, Robespierre regarded 'the people' in general, as opposed to particular individuals, as naturally good and capable of 'virtue'. By 'virtue' he meant love of country *(la patrie)* and the identification of public and private interests. For Robespierre, the 'nation' and the 'people' were interchangeable terms, since the nation was simply the practical expression of the sovereignty of the people: a Republic of free men with equality of rights (154; 148; 149).

Before entering the Committee of Public Safety in August 1793, and indeed for long afterwards, Robespierre had built a formidable reputation as a political tactician, an orator and a champion of the underprivileged, albeit a somewhat pompous and humourless one [doc. 21]. He had defended the liberty of the press, strongly urged a democratic franchise and taken up the cause of Jews, actors, Negro slaves and other minorities. Robespierre had also argued for as much direct democracy as possible, insisting in 1792 that the popular societies of the *sans culottes* were necessary to diffuse 'public spirit' and experience of democratic politics (150). What eventually separated him from the *enragés,* the Hébertists and many others at the grass roots of the popular movement was that he tended to see equality in purely political terms. For Robespierre, like all his colleagues in the C.P.S. with the possible exception of Collot d'Herbois, had little intimate knowledge of the lives of the common people, still less of the poor. As Soboul points out, Robespierre, although a sincere democrat, 'felt ill at ease among the people. A man of the Assembly and the Jacobin Club, he lacked any real feeling for mass action' (150).

Following Rousseau, he disliked great inequalities of wealth and approved of diatribes against the rich, but his own economic ideas were primitive and unsystematic, and he was too much a product of the *bourgeoisie* to reject property as the basis of the social order. Even so, his draft Declaration of Rights in 1793, more radical than the final version, shows that he was willing to go further in the direction of economic equality than the moderate members of the Convention. However, the fact that so many of the *menu peuple* cared more for the price of bread and the level of wages than for the processes of law and the life of Republican virtue exasperated him. He regarded men like Roux and Varlet as little more than ruffians who exploited the people by appealing to the base demands of their bellies **(149; 150; 170**, ch. 6).

From the autumn of 1793 the exigencies of power caused Robespierre to modify his Rousseauist views, indeed to go beyond them. From being a stern critic of the powers of government, he became an advocate of the supremacy of the Convention and the Committee of Public Safety. In his speech of 25 December 1793, Robespierre admitted that constitutional principles could not be executed literally and that a government 'Revolutionary until the peace' had to wield much more executive authority than one in peacetime [**doc. 23**]. Yet the purged Convention was clearly representative only of a minority of Montagnards; even the popular movement had begun to fragment. Hence the legislature as an expression of Rousseau's 'general will' became still more of an abstraction. In his desire to consolidate the Revolutionary government, Robespierre was instrumental in reducing the role and influence of the popular societies after December 1793 and clearing the way for the monolithic government machine. He fully supported the brake which the C.P.S. put on the 'anarchic' Terror and local initiative by the law of 14 Frimaire (14 December)1793. This solidly founded the central Revolutionary dictatorship by preventing the *représentants en mission* from delegating their powers without prior approval from Paris, by abolishing the provincial *armées révolutionnaires*, by putting departmental, district and communal institutions under the inspection of 'national agents' of the C.P.S. and the C.G.S., and by forbidding any independent taxes or loans at a local level. Thus the Republic was given a more rigorous and powerful bureaucracy than any eighteenth century monarchy **(1**, no. 53; **24**, table p. 377). Furthermore, Robespierre was the main opponent of the 'anarchic' dechristianisation campaign, for he had always supported religious toleration and regarded atheism as aristocratic and counter-revolutionary. Dechristianisers must be enemies of France because of the way they sowed division and antagonisms.

So far as Robespierre was concerned, government dictatorship and

Terror were vital to the safety of the Republic. If it were necessary to use violence against the enemies of the people, then his legalistic mind preferred judicial violence by the government rather than the indiscriminate and uncontrolled violence of popular *émeutes* like the September Massacres of 1792. Bound up with his conception of Terror and Republican virtue was commitment to the war. Patriotism was the other side of the coin of virtue. The war which France was waging must be one of principle rather than gain, a war for justice and liberty rather than conquest. A war against tyrants must be fought to the death. By arguing along these lines, Robespierre came close to accepting the war ideology for which he had denounced the Girondins in 1792. Such nationalism owed nothing to Rousseau, while the increasing exploitation of foreign territories made the arguments look even more threadbare [doc. 18].

Opponents of Robespierre, both at the time and since, have made other criticisms. In a situation of conflicting minorities, the conception of the general will and sovereignty of the people seemed increasingly tenuous. There was so much evidence of corruption and factional struggle that Robespierre more and more came to see the general will as an 'ideal' will that had, if necessary, to be ·imposed on people. If virtue failed to emerge spontaneously from below, then it must be imposed from above. The 'people' became in fact a smaller and smaller minority. Early in the Revolution, Robespierre had spoken of the 'people' as opposed to the privileged classes. By 1794 the 'people' meant those who supported the Revolutionary government. All the others were enemies of the Republic, eager to swamp civic virtue in a sea of corruption. On 5 December 1793 he had asserted that 'all reasonable and magnanimous men are on the side of the Republic; all perfidious and corrupt individuals belong to the faction of tyrants'. So the ideal general will emerged from a small minority of virtuous Republicans and patriots: the C.P.S. and its Jacobin supporters. Hence the need for successive purges of false and corrupt factions; that is, all who spoke against the Revolutionary dictatorship, whatever their previous record of Revolutionary orthodoxy.

In this way, Robespierre came close to developing the theory of a Revolutionary élite, a vanguard like Lenin's Bolsheviks. But he lacked both the cynicism and the brutality of a Stalin or a Hitler. There is no reason to doubt that he aimed at political liberty and regarded the Revolutionary dictatorship as temporary in a time of crisis. Although Robespierre can be regarded, in Aulard's phrase, as 'the high priest of political orthodoxy', he was not the personal tyrant depicted by his opponents at Thermidor. He exercised no dominant authority in the

Committee of Public Safety; Barère, Carnot and Prieur signed many more decrees than he did. Nor does he bear sole responsibility for the intensive Terror of 1794. Robespierre had been a determined opponent of capital punishment in 1789 and even in 1794 looked with distaste on what he termed 'guillotine sickness'. While he agreed that enemies of the people deserved death, he revoked a good many arrests and sentences and was never as severe as either the members of the Committee of General Security or his merciless and repulsive young colleague Saint-Just, the 'angel of death' **(170, ch. 10)**.

During the spring and summer of 1794 the Revolutionary government launched a massive propaganda campaign, which included strict control of the press and the theatre, elaborate festivals of Liberty, Equality, Truth, Justice and Amity, and the cult of the Supreme Being. These were designed to promote a civic religion of humanity which, Robespierre hoped, would wean the people from both the 'superstitions' of Catholicism and the 'immorality' of the cult of Reason, thus bringing about social regeneration and loyalty to the Revolutionary government [**doc. 24**]. Nature was the true priest of the Supreme Being; its temple was the universe. J.L. David, the leading neoclassic artist of the age, was called in to design impressive tableaux and scenic effects for the civic festivals. It soon became apparent, however, that the reign of virtue was inoperable. Officially supported puritan rigour of conduct had little appeal outside Jacobin and government circles, especially when the Republican armies began to push back the enemy. Civic religion and the cult of the Supreme Being always had a certain artificiality, a certain remoteness from daily life, a certain verging on the ridiculous.

Moreover, the Revolutionary government soon lost touch with the masses and came eventually to represent no specific interest but that of its own leaders and officials. That was the price it paid for stemming internal rebellion and foreign armies. By the early months of 1794 it came to believe that it could operate the Terror and win the war without the support of the popular movement and turn the machinery of the Terror against those, both on the right and the left, who voiced any criticism of the Revolutionary dictatorship. The popular societies were therefore proscribed and *sans culotte* artillery units absorbed into the armies on the frontier, well away from Paris **(104, ii, book iv, ch. 2)**. Such a conflict between the government and what it dismissed as 'the factions' was not so much a class struggle, though it contained elements of it, as a conflict about the exercise of power. The *sans culotte* idea of direct democracy, with the people of Paris possessing their own armed force and popular committees with police powers, proved unacceptable to the two great Committees. Popular protest was henceforth reduced to the level of riots and demonstrations. Militants were bought off by being offered jobs in the bureaucracy. The result of this dismissal of the popular movement was the increasing isolation of the government and the spreading of apathy and indifference in the country. The divorce between the Revolutionary government and the popular movement robbed the Revolution of its driving force. As Saint-Just complained: 'The Republic is frozen.'

Beneath the surface of rhetoric by Revolutionary leaders and stage-management by David, there was precious little virtue. The winter of 1793-94 was hard for the poor. Hunger and misery in Paris were rivalled only by the scale of gambling and prostitution. Such a ferment seemed a threat to the prosperous classes and to the stability of the Republic. In Ventôse the government turned on the 'factions'. Hébert and his colleagues, it was alleged, were fomenting popular discontent from their base in the Cordeliers Club and the War Office, although in fact only the Section Marat seemed prepared for insurrection. Such ultra-revolutionaries, charged Robespierre and the leading Jacobins, were attempting to undermine the government by the 'anarchic' aims of dechristianisation, vigorous price controls and death for merchants and dishonest traders. On 23 March the Convention decreed that those criticizing the government and stirring anxiety about food supplies were traitors. Hébert, Vincent, Momoro and the heads of the Parisian *armée révolutionnaire,* Ronsin and Mazuel, were arrested, quickly tried and executed. A number of 'corrupt' deputies followed them.

Although the *sans culottes* were stunned when 'Père Duchesne' went to the guillotine, they did nothing. Anxiety and shocked silence replaced patriotic exaltation and Revolutionary fervour in the Paris sections (**71**, ch. 9). There was in fact no Hébertist party with a genuine alternative programme and the so-called Hébertists were men using the popular movement to further their own personal ambitions. But most *sans culottes* saw the execution of the Hébertists as yet another step in the repression of the popular movement and a denial of the right of insurrection (**106**, book ii, part 3). By acting against Paris and the popular movement, the first major Revolutionary crisis where this happened, the C.P.S. seemed to be acting against the Revolution itself. Partly to forestall charges of being reactionary, the government turned on Danton and the 'Indulgents' a week later. They were accused of moderation, of desiring to end the war, of connections with foreign plotters and financial dealings. Danton's venality was revealed. They were executed on 16 Germinal (5 April), after Danton had been prevented from speaking [**doc. 25**].

If the fall of the Hébertists had rendered the popular movement, or what was left of it, resentful and inarticulate, then the fall of the Dantonists frightened many moderate deputies in the Convention, of which the Dantonists were members (127, ch. 12). Such deputies, as well as the propertied classes in general, had earlier been upset by the laws of Ventôse, whereby Saint-Just proposed that the property of suspects be confiscated by the state and the proceeds given to the poor. Lists of both suspects and poor were to be drawn up by local authorities. This was partly a political manoeuvre, aiming to purchase *sans culotte* loyalty towards a *régime* which was reducing them to a political nullity. The proposals were also intended to help calm growing peasant unrest. In fact very little was done in a systematic way to implement the laws of Ventôse. There were some piecemeal confiscations in about thirty departments, but administration proved too chaotic and the will too lacking for any large-scale transference of wealth. By raising fears for the security of property, without doing anything very much to meet the demands of the poor, the Revolutionary government satisfied nobody and deepened hostility on both sides. It was ominous for its future survival that the Committee of Public Safety was internally divided on the issue (124, ch. 5).

8 Thermidor

The great Committee of Public Safety survived the execution of the Dantonists by a mere 113 days, for in the late spring and early summer of 1794 the Revolutionary government became more isolated and resented. Many began to see it as either the personal dictatorship of Robespierre, or that of the triumvirate of Robespierre, Saint-Just and Couthon. Both views lacked substance, but the fact that they were adopted is testimony to the growing atmosphere of suspicion and panic reminiscent of the Great Fear of 1789 (22, book iv, ch. 2). Jacobin clubs in Paris and in the provinces were in a state of confusion and frequently seethed with intrigue. The Revolutionary government looked formidable on paper, but it broke down completely in some parts of France, like the Ardèche and the Var. The Paris *sans culottes* were angry because of the food shortage and the refusal of the Commune to raise wages. 'We are more miserable than before', declared a labourer in an armaments workshop, 'because we can do nothing with our money and must die of hunger. We are mocked with fine words' **(160)**.

By this time the Revolutionary government had become very much the reign of the bureaucrats. Government offices were full of men with a little education and a mere appearance of *civisme*. Militants were either imprisoned or swamped by the bureaucratic mentality. Initiative was stifled at all levels below that of the great Committees; energy which had formerly gone into the 'anarchic Terror' now tended to be devoted to petty quarrels and personal intrigues between rival officials. In an atmosphere of fear and uncertainty, a dull conformity seemed the most judicious course for many to adopt. Government propaganda on behalf of 'virtue' tended to encourage a defensive hypocrisy at the most, or at the least plain boredom, without doing much to diminish robbery, excess and a good deal of place-seeking and financial corruption. A general fear of 'foreign plots', 'prison plots' and assassinations, partly justified by the presence in Paris of large numbers of foreign spies and prisoners in insecure custody, led to the acceleration of Revolutionary justice. The government seemed to be losing its nerve.

Late in May, government panic was deepened by two attempts on Robespierre's life **(159)**. The great Terror of June and July 1794 represented a frantic attempt to preserve itself by a government which felt the ground slipping beneath its feet. Over 2,500 died in the two months before 9 Thermidor (27 July), more than the total for the previous year (127, ch. 13). These executions were the work of the Paris tribunal, which had a monopoly; even death was centralised. By the law of 22 Prairial, the rights of the accused were whittled away to nothing, as the guillotine worked still faster. Such a bloodbath provoked a general reaction of fear and extreme tension, besides a tendency by many outside the government to regard the Terror as no longer the source of the preservation of the Republic, but the instrument of political faction and of the desire of the members of the government to maintain themselves in power. At the same time, the law of 22 Prairial threatened members of the Convention and intensified the rivalry between the C.P.S. and the C.G.S., for the latter had not been consulted on the law (158; 159).

The atmosphere in Paris in June and July 1794 was a mixture of general moroseness and hostility to the Jacobin dictatorship. As authority became discredited, so hitherto keen Republicans felt lost and disorientated. Until the end of June victory in the war was still uncertain, but on 26 June came the victory of the Republican armies at Fleurus, followed by their entry into Brussels on 8 July. Now that the armies were on the offensive, the Terror no longer had the justification of the needs of national defence. Meanwhile the machinery of the Revolutionary government had practically come to a halt in the provinces. The hesitancy of local authorities encouraged reaction: liberty trees were uprooted, there were refusals to draw up lists of suspects. The growth of brigandage and a general sense of dissolution stimulated irrational panic, where every official saw his enemies around the next corner. The government now, writes Professor Cobb, was acting 'in a bureaucratic vacuum, with a stream of orders echoing down and a stream of echoes pouring up' (106, book ii, part iii, ch. 15). Underneath the official, propaganda-inspired surface of monolithic orthodoxy and unanimity, there was apathy and indifference, disillusionment and boredom. People had had enough of militancy and were ready to return to the workbench, the shop, the family and the *cabaret* (124, ch. 6).

Priests emerged from hiding to encourage resistance to the Terror. Women demonstrated for religion, going on pilgrimages and witnessing miracles in a chiliasm of despair after their privations. The great festival of the Supreme Being in Nôtre-Dame on 20 Prairial (8 June) did little to absorb this resurgence of religious feeling. On the contrary it led to the charge that Robespierre aimed at his own deification and that God was being recruited as a member of the Revolutionary government. Economic discontent was also rife in Paris; a renewed food shortage led to demands for higher wages. Yet the C.P.S. issued a new *maximum* on wages which would mean starvation for many families. A carpenter, for example, would receive 3 francs 15 sous instead of 8 francs. Hence a labour agitation arose which further widened the breach between the government and the common people in the towns (160; 71, ch. 9). At the same time, the peasantry was alienated by the erratic operation of the maximum on grain and consumables.

The power struggle which brought down Robespierre and his associates on 9 Thermidor therefore took place in something of a vacuum, for the common people had lost interest in what they regarded as factional struggles. Popular institutions, like the Paris Commune, had been anaesthetised by being packed full of passive government officials. Robespierre himself almost seemed to desire political suicide. In a state of nervous exhaustion, he absented himself from the C.P.S. in June. The Committee itself began to come apart under the strain of continued internal divisions. Panic became vindictive. In the Convention, moderate members of the 'Plain' felt menaced as the great Terror continued and the number of prisoners in the capital swelled alarmingly (159).

Such an atmosphere of apprehension provided a suitable temperature for the flourishing of plots and rumours of plots. The conspiracy of Fouché, Tallien, Carnot, Collot D'Herbois and their friends to bring down Robespierre had therefore a great deal of tacit support. The Revolutionary government was being ruined by its internal contradictions. Many deputies had never forgiven the militant Montagnards for calling in the *sans culottes* to get rid of the Girondins on 2 June 1793. They had been willing to sanction the power of the great Committees only because of the seriousness of the national crisis, whilst still resenting the domination of the legislative by the executive (159). Although Robespierre spoke fourteen times in eleven sessions at the Jacobin Club, protesting against being labelled a tyrant, he remained full of indecision. Perhaps this was because he sensed the erosion of his old basis of support in the Paris Commune and among the *sans culottes.* Perhaps also he, as well as his close collaborators Saint-Just, Couthon, Le Bas and his brother Augustin, was unable to act decisively because, in the last analysis, he had too much respect for the Convention to defy it openly and try to lead a popular revolt against a hostile majority in the Assembly.

On 8 Thermidor, Robespierre made his last speech in the Convention, denouncing the C.G.S. and the Treasury, denying that he was a dictator, pointing to the danger of a military plot and urging reconciliation. It availed him little, for the next day his enemies closed in on him. Neither Robespierre nor Saint-Just was allowed to speak, amid shouts of 'down with the tyrant!' The Convention decreed the arrest of Robespierre, Saint-Just, Couthon, Le Bas and Augustin Robespierre. Maximilien was taken to the *mairie,* the others to prison, from which they soon escaped to join him. Declared outlaws, they were quickly recaptured, Robespierre being shot, or shooting himself, in the jaw. Next day they were executed with seventeen others (**127**, ch. 15; **170**, ch. 10). A force of 3,000 *sans culottes* had assembled on the Place de Grève on the evening of 9 Thermidor, but had failed to act decisively in an attempt to save 'Saint Maximilien', as he had once been. The soulless Revolutionary government, the maximum on wages, the food shortage, the emasculation or destruction of their political institutions, had drained away their revolutionary zeal. Thus the people of Paris remained passive as Robespierre and his colleagues went to the guillotine, soon to be followed by nearly a hundred 'Robespierrists'. The more prosperous inhabitants of the capital, however, cheered as the bodies were dragged away to a ditch of quicklime.

Within a few weeks, the personnel of the Revolutionary Government had been drastically purged and the machinery of Terror dismantled. The country passed into a determined and savage reaction against Montagnards and terrorists of all shades. The Paris sections were seized by moderates, while the repulsive *jeunesse dorée* spearheaded a witch-hunt with a brutality that rivalled Carrier at Nantes and Fouché at Lyon in the Year II. The 'White Terror' of the Year III (September 1794 to September 1795) frequently took the form of undisciplined murder gangs operating against former terrorists, or rumoured terrorists, in counter-revolutionary areas, especially the south-east. As many persons were murdered in the south-east and the west between 1795 and 1803 as perished during the Terror of the Year II. Many others took refuge in exile or suicide. The 'anarchic' Terror of 1793 was thus replaced by the anarchic White Terror of 1795 (**106**, book ii, part ii).

Inflation was increased by the abandonment of economic controls and continued high war expenditure, leading to still higher food prices. The poor were even worse off than they had been during the Year II. The wealthy classes, on the other hand, profited from inflation and speculation and threw their money about on food, *salons* and high fashion. If virtue had been in short supply during the Jacobin Terror, it was almost entirely absent in the general reaction against 'puritanism' which characterised the Thermidorian *régime.* Half-hearted *sans culotte* risings were put down with cannonfire in Germinal and

Prairial (April and May) 1795, to be followed by savage repression. This left bitter memories, but there was no further popular rising in Paris until 1848 (71, ch. 10).

Montagnards in the Assembly had also been eliminated. From the autumn of 1795 until Napoleon's *coup d'état* of Brumaire (November 1799), the conservative Republic was plagued by instability, as it oscillated from right to left, trying to avoid the extremes of royalism and republican extremism by successive purges, with the aid of the army. By 1797 it was clearly only a matter of time before the army dismissed the civilians and controlled the Republic.

PART FOUR

Assessment

9. The French Revolution and the World

At first sight the French Revolution did not change the country all that much. The nobility was far from being destroyed, for only 1,158 out of 400,000 nobles were executed, while 16,431 emigrated, many only temporarily (126). Thus the majority of noble families remained relatively unaffected by the Revolution and Terror (177). Though the noble share of land-ownership fell, the transfer of property during the Revolution was not as drastic as one might expect. Those who bought the *biens nationaux* and confiscated property of suspects and *émigrés* were usually those who possessed some land already: more often than not the urban bourgeoisie (29; 33). The Church also survived, benefiting from a strong religious reaction after Thermidor. By the 1801 Concordat between the Pope and Napoleon, the Roman Catholic Church became the religion 'of the majority of Frenchmen'. Political democracy was swept away in France for half a century and by 1815 the Bourbons were back.

Yet William Wordsworth was right when, in his unpublished *Reply to the Bishop of Llandaff* in 1793, he described the Revolution as 'a convulsion from which is to spring a fairer order of things'. Divine right monarchy had gone for good. So had the old arbitrary and hierarchical society. Although the Church survived, it never regained its old status and authority, partly because its economic power had been permanently eroded by the Revolution. Neither did a restored nobility fully regain their position in society. After 1795, France possessed a more open and fluid society where careers were much more open to talent and ownership of property was more diffused. The power of the press and public opinion was henceforth acknowledged. Conflicts in the countryside were less intense than before 1789. On the other hand the violence of the Revolution, especially in the Year II, left France badly divided and almost impossible to govern. The instability of French government in the nineteenth and twentieth centuries owes a good deal to the antagonisms and tensions created both by the Revolution itself and by the myths which grew up about it after Thermidor.

The French Revolution posed a vigorous and aggressive challenge to the western world in the late eighteenth and early nineteenth centuries.

The Jacobin Republic of 1792-94 provided a model of a determined militant minority implementing the idea of the total sovereignty of the people; a model which was to inspire popular agitations inside and outside France, both nationalist and socialist. In the Thermidorian period. Babeuf developed primitive socialist theories which were to link Jacobinism with nineteenth-century socialism. The constitutional Revolution of 1789-92 provided a model of restricted, property-owning political democracy which helped to inspire European middle-class liberalism in the nineteenth century. The example of the *sans culottes* and the Revolutionary *journées* inspired oppressed peoples to seek their own versions of direct democracy and popular sovereignty. At the same time it prompted rulers, nobles and the clergy to unite in defence of the status quo. Reforming monarchs and enlightened despots quickly disappeared when fears of the contagious 'French epidemic' proved potent.

Whatever the strength of the forces of reaction in both France and Europe after the end of the Revolutionary and Napoleonic Wars in 1815, there was much that could never be erased. Warfare itself was put on a new footing; the intricate manoeuvring of the eighteenth-century battlefield had passed away. Democracy and popular nationalism remained basic forces in both the nineteenth and twentieth centuries. Modern political parties and class conflict both have their origins in the French Revolution. So do liberal democracy, communism and fascism. The increased power of wealth, as opposed to birth, in post-industrial society can be traced to the same source (**66**). For all these reasons, the French Revolution can still be seen as Professor R.R. Palmer saw it in the dark days of 1941: 'the crossroads of the modern world' (**127**, ch. 15).

PART FIVE

Documents

The effects of rural poverty in 1789

The following extracts from four of the 25,000 'cahiers de doléances' illustrate the tensions created at the bottom of rural society by the economic crisis of the late 1780s and help to explain the peasant risings and the 'Great Fear'.

[a] *Rural degeneracy in Pleurs, Bailliage de Sézanne*

Afflicted by so many misfortunes and suffering from poverty, the people of the countryside have become listless; they have fallen into a state of numbness, a kind of apathy, which is the most dangerous of all complaints and the most disastrous for the prosperity of a country. The population is suffering. They are afraid to get married, for marriage only holds the prospect of further hardships; they would immediately be taxed, asked for road services or charges (*corvées*), for labour services and contributions of all kinds. They fear a situation where their family would be a burden on them, since they can only anticipate their children being poor and wretched.

Oh petty tyrants placed at the heart of the provinces to hold sway over their destinies! Oh proprietors of seigneurial estates who demand the most crippling and servile exactions! Oh rich citizens who own property for the moment! Be so good as to leave for a time your palaces and *châteaux,* leave your towns where you have created new problems, where you are offered with both hands everything that indulgence and luxury artisans can invent to stimulate your blunted senses, your satiated spirits; be so good as to glance at those unfortunate men whose muscles are only occupied in working for you! What do you see in our villages, in our fields? A few enfeebled men, whose pale faces are withered by poverty and shame, their wives lamenting their fecundity, each child wearing rags.

Among them, however, you will find several who are happy; these seem to be men of a different kind; they are in fact privileged men like you, nourished on the food of the people; they live amid abundance and each day is pure and serene for them. Such a striking comparison has served to deepen the misery of the labourer, if he is at all sensitive.

[b] *Robbery and pillage in Lugny-Champagne, Bailliage de Bourges*

The inhabitants of the parish of Lugny-Champagne are complaining that at the beginning of the harvest time there arrived in the district a huge number of male and female gleaners from other areas, who flooded into fields that were still covered with sheaves and spread themselves everywhere, even among the fields not yet harvested; the men in charge of the fields could not get them out; not only did they glean among the sheaves, but they seized fistsful of grain from the sheaves themselves; if the farmer tried to say anything, they poured abuse on him; they even chased away the very poor of the village. To guard against such inconvenience, the inhabitants want no itinerants to be allowed to glean, because young men and women are then unwilling to do the work, even at high wages; and as for those who are not travellers, like widows, poor women and their children, they must only be permitted to glean if they have a certificate of good character signed by their priest.

[c] *Vagabonds in Marsainvilliers and Chaon, Bailliage d'Orléans*

It is not possible for the inhabitants of Marsainvilliers to arrest the beggars; that would be to expose them to frequent attack, even to gunfire. The inhabitants of Chaon are angry when they see so many wretches cast themselves on public charity and thus take the money due to the genuine poor; often they enrich themselves, under the cloak of poverty, and having thus spent their lives...die opulent and leave small fortunes to the children they have brought up in idleness and mendicity.

French texts in P. Goubert and M. Denis, eds, *1789 Les Français ont la parole: cahiers des États Généraux*, Paris, Julliard, 1964

document 2

The overthrow of feudalism

This complaint to the National Assembly on 20 August 1789 shows how, in many parts of the country, peasants took violent action against the feudal régime.

. . . On 29 July 1789, a group of brigands from elsewhere, together with my vassals and those of Vrigni, the next parish to mine, two hundred in all, came to my *château* at Sassy, parish of Saint Christopher, near Argentan, and, after breaking the locks on the cupboards containing my title deeds, they seized the registers which could be so necessary to me and took them away, or burned them in the woods near my *château;* my guard was unable to offer any resistance, being the only warden in this area, where I myself do not reside. These wretched people had the tocsin rung in neighbouring parishes in order to swell their numbers. I am all the more sad about this loss because I have never let my vassals feel the odious weight of ancient feudalism, of which I am sure they could be redeemed in present circumstances; but who will ever be able to certify and prove the damage that they have inflicted on my property? I appeal to your discretion to bring in some law whereby the National Assembly can reimburse me for my loss, above all for the use of common land, as useful to my parishioners as to my own estate, whose title deeds they burned. I will not take steps against those whom I know to have been with the brigands who, not content with burning my papers, have killed all my pigeons. But I expect full justice in the spirit of equity which guides you, and which gives me the greatest confidence.

COMTE DE GERMINY

P. Sagnac and P. Caron, *Les Comités de droits féodaux et de législation et l'abolition du régime seigneurial 1789-1793,* Paris, 1907, p. 158.

document 3
The declaration of the rights of man and the citizen 1789

Very much the charter of the 'patriot' educated middle classes who led the Revolution.

The representatives of the French people, sitting in the National Assembly considering that ignorance of, neglect of, and contempt for the rights of man are the sole causes of public misfortune and the corruption of governments, have resolved to set out in a solemn declaration the natural, inalienable and sacred rights of man, in order that this declaration, constantly before all members of the civic body, will constantly remind them of their rights and duties, in order that acts of legislative and executive power can be frequently compared with the purpose of every political institution, thus making them more respected; in order that the demands of the citizens, henceforth founded on simple and irrefutable principles, will always tend towards the maintenance of the constitution and the happiness of everyone.

Consequently the National Assembly recognises and declares, in the presence of, and under the auspices of, the Supreme Being, the following rights of man and of the citizen:

i   Men are born and remain free and equal in rights. Social distinctions can only be founded on communal utility.

ii   The purpose of all political associations is the preservation of the natural and imprescriptible rights of man. These rights are liberty, property, security and resistance to oppression.

iii   The principle of all sovereignity emanates essentially from the nation. No group of men, no individual, can exercise any authority which does not specifically emanate from it.

iv   Liberty consists in being able to do whatever does not harm others. Hence the exercise of the natural rights of every man is limited only by the need for other members of society to exercise the same rights. These limits can only be determined by the law.

v   The law only has the right to prohibit actions harmful to society. What is not prohibited by law cannot be forbidden, and nobody can be forced to do what the law does not require.

vi   The law is the expression of the general will. All citizens have the right to take part personally, or through their representatives, in the making of the law. It should be the same for everyone, whether it protects or punishes. All citizens, being equal in the eyes of the law, are equally admissible to all honours, offices and public employment, according to their capacity and without any distinction other than those of their integrity and talents.

vii   A man can only be accused, arrested or detained in cases determined by law, and according to the procedure it requires. Those who solicit, encourage, execute, or cause to be executed, arbitrary orders must be punished, but every citizen called upon or arrested in the name of the law must obey instantly; resistance renders him culpable.

viii   The law must only require punishments that are strictly and evidently necessary, and a person can only be punished according to an established law passed before the offence and legally applied.

ix   Every man being presumed innocent until he has been declared guilty, if it is necessary to arrest him, all severity beyond what is necessary to secure his arrest shall be severely punished by law.

x   No man ought to be uneasy about his opinions, even his religious beliefs, provided that their manifestation does not interfere with the public order established by the law.

xi   The free communication of thought and opinion is one of the most precious rights of man: every citizen can therefore talk, write and publish freely, except that he is responsible for abuses of this liberty in cases determined by the law.

xii   The guaranteeing of the rights of man and the citizen requires a public force: this force is therefore established for everybody's advantage and not for the particular benefit of the persons who are entrusted with it.

xiii   A common contribution is necessary for the maintenance of the public force and for administrative expenses; it must be equally apportioned between all citizens, according to their means.

xiv   All citizens have the right, personally or by means of their representatives, to have demonstrated to them the necessity of public taxes, so that they can consent freely to them, can check how they are used, and can determine the shares to be paid, their assessment, collection and duration.

xv   The community has the right to hold accountable every public official in its administration.

xvi   Every society which has no assured guarantee of rights, nor a separation of powers, does not possess a constitution.

xvii   Property being a sacred and inviolable right, nobody can be deprived of it, except when the public interest, legally defined, evidently requires it, and then on condition there is just compensation in advance.

French text in J.M. Thompson, *French Revolution Documents 1789-94,* Blackwell 1933, pp. 109-11.

document 4

The 'problème des subsistances' 1789

Bailly, a distinguished mathematician and astronomer, was one of the popular heroes of 1789. The first president of the National Assembly, he became Mayor of Paris on 15 July. His diary reveals the enormity of the problem of supplying the Paris market with food and the accepted link between bread and insurrection.

26 August: I have already demanded that attention be devoted to the provisioning of Paris with grain. I returned today to the Assembly, and I asked that attention be given to providing the capital with food for the early winter months, observing that we can only obtain it from foreign sources. I saw that the grain bought by the government is running out. I thought that in a disastrous period, at the time of a good harvest, but one which will start being consumed two or three months earlier than usual, it was necessary to have a stockpile of food in reserve, to prevent any cause for, or pretext for, an insurrection and that such a stockpile could only be obtained abroad. . . . The cartloads of flour in our convoys are not only pillaged on the way by mobs, but are also pillaged in Paris by bakers who wait for them in the *faubourgs* . . . such disorder creates two serious problems: the first is that the distribution of flour is unequal: one baker has too much, another not enough; the second is that the Paris Market is poorly stocked, which disturbs public opinion.

Mémoires de Bailly, Paris, 1821-22, ii, 304-5.

The clerical oath, 27 November 1790

The National Assembly . . . decrees as follows:

i   The bishops, former archbishops, and *curés* still in office, will be required, if they have not already done so, to take the oath . . . they will swear . . . carefully to look after the faithful of the diocese, or of the parish with which they have been entrusted; to be faithful to the nation, to the law and to the king, and to preserve with all their power the constitution which has been decreed by the National Assembly and accepted by the king . . . .

viii We will pursue, as violators of public order, and punish according to the rigours of the law, all ecclesiastical and lay persons who combine together in order to refuse to obey the decrees of the National Assembly, accepted and sanctioned by the king, or who try to form or arouse opposition to their execution.

French text in Thompson, *op. cit.*, pp. 80-2.

The influence of the Jacobin Club 1791

From May 1789 'patriots' came together to discuss political problems. This was the origin of the political clubs, including the Breton Club. After October 1789 it met in the old Jacobin monastery in the Rue St Honoré as the 'Société des Amis de la Constitution', now open to the middle classes generally as well as deputies. It soon became known as the Jacobin Club and corresponded with clubs founded in the principal provincial towns. This report is from Camille Desmoulins's brilliant weekly paper.

In the propagation of patriotism, that is to say of philanthropy, this new religion which is bound to conquer the universe, the club or church of the Jacobins seems destined for the same primacy as that of the church of Rome in the propagation of Christianity. Already all the clubs and assemblies and churches of patriots, which are being formed everywhere, demand correspondence with it and write to it as a sign of fraternity. ... The Jacobin Society is truly the committee of inquiry of the nation, less dangerous to good citizens than that of the National Assembly, because the denunciations, the deliberations are public there; much more formidable to bad citizens, because it covers by its correspondence with affiliated societies all the nooks and crannies of the 83 *départements*. Not only is it the great investigator which terrifies the aristocrats; it is also the great investigator which redresses all abuses and comes to the aid of all citizens. It seems that in reality the club acts as a public ministry alongside the National Assembly. They come from everywhere to place the grievances of the oppressed at its feet, before taking their complaints to the worthy Assembly. In the assembly hall of the Jacobins flow increasingly deputations, missions of congratulation, those seeking close relations with the club, those seeking to promote vigilance, or those seeking the redress of injustices.

Les Révolutions de France èt de Brabant, 14 February 1791.

document 7

The overthrow of the monarchy: 10 August 1792

This letter, sent by a National Guard to a friend in Rennes, describes the events of the 10 August and the following days. Despite being from the point of view of a participant, it keeps a reasonably objective tone.

Paris — 11 August 1792 — Year 4 of Liberty
We are all tired out, doubtless less from spending two nights under arms than from heartache. Men's spirits were stirred after the unfortunate decree which whitewashed Lafayette. Nevertheless, we had a quiet enough evening; a group of *fédérés* from Marseille gaily chanted patriotic songs in the Beaucaire café, the refreshment room of the National Assembly. It was rumoured 'Tonight the tocsin will ring, the alarm drum will be beaten. All the *faubourgs* will burst into insurrection, supported by 6,000 *fédérés*.' At 11 o'clock we go home, at the same instant as the drums call us back to arms. We speed from our quarters and our battalion, headed by two pieces of artillery, marches to the palace. Hardly have we reached the garden of the Tuileries than we hear the alarm cannon. The alarm drum resounds through all the streets of

Paris. People run for arms from all over the place. Soon the public squares, the new bridge, the main thoroughfares, are covered with troops. The National Assembly, which had finished its debate early, was recalled to its duties. It only knew of some of the preparations which had been made for the *Journée* of 10 August. First the commandant of the palace wishes to hold the mayor a hostage there, then he sends him to the mayor's office. The people fear a display of his talents! In the general council of the Commune it is decreed that, according to the wishes of the forty-eight sections, it is no longer necessary to recognise the constituted authorities if dethronement is not immediately announced and new municipal bodies, keeping Pétion and Manuel at their head, entrusted with popular authority. However, the *faubourgs* organised themselves into an army and placed in their centre Bretons, Marseillais and Bordelais, and all the other *fédérés.* More than 20,000 men march across Paris, bristling with pikes and bayonets. Santerre had been obliged to take command of them. The National Assembly are told that the army has broken into the palace. All hearts are frozen. Discussion is provoked again by the question of the safety of the king, when it is learned that Louis XVI seeks refuge in the bosom of the Assembly.

Forty-eight members are sent to the palace. The royal family places itself in the middle of the deputation. The people fling bitter reproaches at the king and accuse him of being the author of his troubles. Hardly was the king safe than the noise of cannon-fire increased. The Breton *fédérés* beat a tattoo. Some officers suggested retreat to the commander of the Swiss guards. But he seemed prepared and soon, by a clever tactic, captured the artillery which the National Guard held in the courtyard. These guns, now turned on the people, fire and strike them down. But soon the conflict is intensified everywhere. The Swiss, surrounded, overpowered, stricken, then run out of ammunition. They plea for mercy, but it is impossible to calm the people, furious at Helvetian treachery.

The Swiss were cut to pieces. Some were killed in the state-rooms, others in the garden. Many died on the Champs-Elysees. Heavens! That Liberty should cost Frenchmen blood and tears! How many victims there were among both the People and the National Guard! The total number of dead could run to 2,000. All the Swiss who had been taken prisoner were escorted to the Place de Grève. There they had their brains blown out. They were traitors sacrificed to vengeance. What vengeance! I shivered to the roots of my being. At least 47 heads were cut off. The Grève was littered with corpses, and heads were paraded on the ends of several pikes. The first heads to be severed were those of seven *chevaliers du poignard,* slain at eight o'clock in the morning on the Place Vendôme. Many Marseillais perished in the *journée* of 10 August. Their second-in-command was killed, so was the commander of the Bretons.

The bronze statues in the Place Royale, Place Vendôme, Place Louis XIV, Place Louis XV, are thrown to the ground. The Swiss are pursued everywhere. The National Assembly, the department and the municipality are in permanent session. ... People are still far from calm and it will be difficult to re-establish order. However, we see peace starting to re-appear. The king and his family have passed the night in the porter's lodging of the National Assembly.

Tonight the National Assembly has decreed [the creation of] the National Convention. The electors are gathered in primary assemblies to select deputies. They only need to be twenty-five years old and have a residence qualification. It appears that the *coup* of 10 August has forestalled one by the aristocracy. One realizes now that the Swiss are the victims of their credulity, that they hoped for support, but that the rich men who should have fought with them dared not put in an appearance. We have been told that there are 8,000 royalist grenadiers in Paris. These 8,000 citizens seem to have stayed at home. Only one equestrian statue has been preserved in the capital: that of Henri IV.

MS letter in John Rylands Library, University of Manchester.

document 8

La Vendée 1793

This report by two refugees from Saint-Pierre-de-Chemillé describes a typical band of Vendéan rebels.

Wednesday, 13 March, about 5 in the afternoon, a large number of men in a band, armed with guns, hooks, forks, scythes and so on, all wearing white cockades and decorated with small, square, cloth medallions, on which are embroidered different shapes, such as crosses, little hearts pierced with pikes, and other signs of that kind, appeared in the township of Saint-Pierre. All these fellows shouted 'Long live the King and our Good Priests! We want our king, our priests and the old régime!' And they wanted to kill off all the patriots, especially us two witnesses. All that band, which was terrifyingly large, hurled itself at the Patriots, who had gathered to resist their attempt, they killed many, made many others prisoner, and scattered the rest.

Archives départementales, Maine-et-Loire, K1018.

document 9

Levée en masse: 23 August 1793
This decree marks the appearance of total war.

i   From this time, until the enemies of France have been expelled from the territory of the Republic, all Frenchmen are in a state of permanent requisition for the army. The young men will go to fight; married men will forge arms and transport food and supplies; women will make tents and uniforms and work in hospitals; children will find old rags for bandages; old men will appear in public places to excite the courage of warriors, the hatred of kings, and the unity of the Republic.

ii   Public buildings will be converted into barracks, public squares into armament workshops, the soil of cellars will be washed to extract saltpetre.

iii   Rifles will be confined exclusively to those who march to fight the enemy; military service in the interior will be performed with sporting guns and side-arms.

iv   Riding horses will be requisitioned for the cavalry corps; draught horses, other than those used in agriculture, will pull artillery and stores.

v   The Committee of Public Safety is charged with the taking of all measures to establish, without delay, an extraordinary factory for arms of all kinds, to cater for the determination and energy of the French people; it is consequently authorised to form as many establishments, factories, workshops and mills as are necessary to carry out the work, as well as requiring, for this purpose, throughout the Republic, craftsmen and workers who can contribute to its success; for this object there is a sum of 30 millions at the disposal of the ministry of war... French text in Thompson, *op. cit.*, pp. 255-6.

What is a *sans culotte?*

This document represents the 'sans culottes's' view of themselves' 'L'Ami des Lois' was a fashionable comedy of 1793, 'Chaste Susanne' a light operetta; Gorsas was a Girondin journalist; 'La Chronique' and 'Patriot Français' were Girondin newspapers.

A *sans culotte*, you rogues? He is someone who always goes about on foot, who has not got the millions you would all like to have, who has no châteaux, no valets to wait on him, and who lives simply with his wife and children, if he has any, on the fourth or fifth storey. He is useful because he knows how to till a field, to forge iron, to use a saw, to roof a house, to make shoes, and to spill his blood to the last drop for the safety of the Republic. And because he is a worker, you are sure not to meet his person in the Café de Chartres, or in the gaming houses where others plot and wager, nor in the National Theatre, where *L'Ami des Lois* is performed, nor in the Vaudeville Theatre at a performance of *Chaste Susanne,* nor in the literary clubs where for two sous, which are so precious to him, you are offered Gorsas's muck, with the *Chronique* and the *Patriot Français.*

In the evening he goes to the assembly of his Section, not powdered and perfumed and nattily booted, in the hope of being noticed by the citizenesses in the galleries, but ready to support sound proposals with all his might and ready to pulverise those which come from the despised faction of politicians.

Finally, a *sans culotte* always has his sabre well-sharpened, ready to cut off the ears of all opponents of the Revolution; sometimes he carries his pike about with him; but as soon as the drum beats you see him leave for the Vendée, for the Army of the Alps, or for the Army of the North.

Archives Nationales, F7 4775/48, dossier Vinternier.

A *sans culotte* definition of a *feuillant,* an aristocrat and a moderate

This document shows who the 'sans culottes' regarded as enemies of the people. Note the political definition of 'aristocrat'.

The aristocrat is a man who, because of his scorn or indifference, has not been entered on the register of National Guards and who has not taken the civic oath. ... He is a man who, by his conduct, his activities, his speeches and his writings, as well as by his connections, has given proof that he bitterly regrets the passing of the *ancien régime* and despises every aspect of the Revolution. He is a man whose conduct suggests that he would send cash to the *émigrés* or join the enemy army, if only he had the means to do the one and the opportunity to do the other. He is a man who has always despaired of the triumph of the Revolution, who has spread bad news which is obviously false. He is a man who by inefficient management has left land uncultivated, without letting any to farmers or selling any at a fair price. He is a man who has not purchased any national wealth *(biens nationnaux)* whilst having both the resources and the opportunity. Above all, he is a man who declared that he would not buy them and advised others not to perform this act of civic duty. He is a man who, though he has the resources and the opportunity, has not provided work for journeymen and workmen at a wage level above that of the price of basic necessities. He is a man who has not subscribed to the fund for the Volunteers, and certainly has not given as much as he could. He is a man who, because of aristocratic pride, does not visit the civil clergy, and what is more has advised others not to do so. He is a man who has done nothing to ameliorate the lives of the poor and who does not wear a cockade of three inches circumference; a man who has bought clothes other than national dress and who takes no pride in the title and clothing of a *sans culotte.* The true language of the Republic assures you that this definition is just and that the true patriot has done quite the opposite for the well-being of the Republic.
Archives Nationales, D x1 23, d,77, p. 35, May 1793.

The *sans culotte* **programme**

The following address, sent to the Convention by the 'Section des Sans Culottes' on 2 September 1793, summarises the social and economic aims of the more extreme 'sans culottes' and marks the nearest they came to a concrete programme of social equality.

Mandatories of the People — Just how long are you going to tolerate royalism, ambition, egotism, intrigue and avarice, each of them linked to fanaticism, and opening our frontiers to tyranny, whilst spreading devastation and death everywhere? How long are you going to suffer food-hoarders spreading famine throughout the Republic in the detestable hope that patriots will cut each other's throats and the throne will be restored over our bloody corpses, with the help of foreign despots? You must hurry for there is no time to lose... the whole universe is watching you: humanity reproaches you for the troubles which are devastating the French Republic. Posterity will damn your names in future if you do not speedily find a remedy. ... You must hurry, representatives of the people, to deprive all former nobles, priests, *parlementaires* and financiers of all administrative and judicial responsibility; also to fix the price of basic foodstuffs, raw materials, wages, and the profits of industry and commerce. You have both the justification and the power to do so. To speak plainly! To talk of aristocrats, royalists, moderates and counter-revolutionaries is to draw attention to property rights, held to be sacred and inviolable ... no doubt; but do these rogues ignore the fact that property rights are confined to the extent of the satisfaction of physical needs? Don't they know that nobody has the right to do anything that will injure another person? What could be more harmful than the arbitrary power to increase the price of basic necessities to a level beyond the means of seven eighths of the citizens? ... Do they not realize that every individual in the Republic must employ his intelligence and the strength of his arms in the service of the Republic, and must spill his blood for her to the very last drop? In return, the Republic should guarantee to each citizen the means of obtaining sufficient basic necessities to stay alive.

Would you not agree that we have passed a harsh law

against hoarders? Representatives of the people, do not let the law be abused. ... This law, which forces those with large stocks of foodstuffs to declare their hoard, tends to favour hoarders more than it wipes out hoarding; it puts all their stocks under the supervision of the nation, yet permits them to charge whatever price their greed dictates. Consequently, the general assembly of the *Section des Sans Culottes* considers it to be the duty of all citizens to propose measures which seem likely to bring about a return of abundance and public tranquillity. It therefore resolves to ask the Convention to decree the following:

1. That former nobles will be barred from military careers and every kind of public office; that former *parlementaires,* priests and financiers will be deprived of all administrative and judicial duties.
2. That the price of basic necessities be fixed at the levels of 1789-90, allowing for differences in quality.
3. That the price of raw materials, level of wages and profits of industry and commerce also be fixed, so that the hard-working man, the cultivator and the trader will be able to procure basic necessities, and also those things which add to their enjoyment.
4. That all those cultivators who, by some accident, have not been able to harvest their crop, be compensated from public funds.
5. That each department be allowed sufficient public money to ensure that the price of basic foodstuffs will be the same for all citizens of the Republic.
6. That the sums of money allowed to departments be used to eradicate variations in the price of foodstuffs and necessities and in the cost of transporting them to all parts of the Republic, so that each citizen is equal in these things.
7. That existing leases be cancelled and rents fixed at the levels of 1789-90, as for foodstuffs.
8. That there be a fixed maximum on personal wealth.
9. That no single individual shall possess more than the declared maximum.
10. That nobody be able to lease more land than is necessary for a fixed number of ploughs.
11. That no citizen shall possess more than one workshop or retail shop.

12. That all who possess goods and land without legal title be recognised as proprietors.

The *Section des Sans Culottes* thinks that these measures will create abundance and tranquillity, and will, little by little, remove the gross inequalities of wealth and multiply the number of proprietors.

Bibliothèque Nationale, Lb/40 2140.

document 13

The law of suspects 1793

This law, passed on the 17 September, cast the net of suspicion very wide indeed and was partly a response to *sans culotte* demands.

1. Immediately after the publication of this decree, all suspects found on the territory of the Republic and who are still at liberty will be arrested.

2. Suspects are (i) Those who, either by their conduct or their relationships, by their conversation or by their writing, are shown to be partisans of tyranny and federalism and enemies of liberty; (ii) Those who cannot justify, under the provisions of the law of 21 March last, their means of existence and the performance of their civic duties; (iii) Those have been refused certificates of civic responsibility; (iv) Public officials suspended or deprived of their functions by the National Convention or its agents, and not since reinstated, especially those who have been, or ought to be, dismissed by the law of 12 August last; (v) Those former nobles, including husbands, wives, fathers, mothers, sons or daughters, brothers or sisters, and agents of *émigrés,* who have not constantly manifested their loyalty to the Revolution; (vi) Those who have emigrated during the interval between the 1 July 1789 and the publication of the law of 8 April 1792, although they may have returned to France during the period of delay fixed by the law or before.

The *comités de surveillance* established under the law of 21 March last, or those substituting for them, are empowered by the decrees of the representatives of the people to go to the armies and the departments, according to the particular decrees of the National Convention, and are charged with drawing up, in each local district, a list of suspects, of issuing arrest warrants against them, and of affixing seals to their private papers. The commanders of the public force, to whom these arrest warrants will be conveyed, must carry them out immediately, on pain of dismissal.

French text in Thompson, *op. cit.,* pp. 258-9.

document 14

The blade of vengeance

This petition to the Convention from the William Tell section of Paris, dated 12 November 1793, illustrates the endorsement of the Terror by the militant 'sans culottes'.

[The execution of Marie Antoinette and the Girondin deputies] furnished a terrible example to astonish the universe and strike fear amongst the most guilty. Bloodshed is necessary in order to punish those who might follow their example. Representatives of the people, it will take more than the deaths of a fistful of conspirators to destroy all the strands of the most abominable plot to hatch in human breasts; there must be a public sacrifice of traitors to heal the wounds of a country slaughtered by its disfigured children. The aristocracy has not given up its shadowy and sinister plotting. Murder and carnage are its favourite foods; the fall of 21 heads [on 16 and 31 October 1793], that of the slut Marie Antoinette and the dissolute inhabitants of the palace of hell, has highlighted aristocratic fury and revealed in a flash its intention of knocking over the column of liberty. There are other enemies no less dangerous: the evil public robbers and plunderers. Legislators! Do not spare those vampires who suck the blood of *La Patrie;* scrutinise carefully the scandalous fortunes which remain an insult to the poverty of the people, and only close the graveyards when our most evil internal enemies have been swallowed up. Representatives, the days of forgiveness are now past; the blade of vengeance should fall on all guilty heads; the people await drastic measures which will make sure that the guilty are not spared. Do not forget the sublime words of the prophet Marat: Sacrifice two hundred thousand heads and you will save a million.

Archives Nationales, C280, pl. 769, p. 38.

The armée revolutionnaire at Caen

This letter from a Parisian 'cannonier' of the 'Section du Bon-Conseil', serving in a detachment of the 'armée révolutionnaire' at Caen, reveals the desire for vengeance felt by the members of the 'armées' and their constant fear of assassination, though few, if any, were in fact assassinated. Thus they felt themselves to be 'martyrs of liberty'. Charlotte Corday, from Caen, murdered Marat on 13 July 1793.

I have no pity for the enemies of my country; they have spilled, and continue to spill, the blood of my brothers, who all demand vengeance, and those who have played the part of counter-revolutionaries deserve death at angry hands. ... I have just been through the department of Calvados, which is far from being fully republicanised ... there (in the commune of Caen) I fancy I saw all the knives of the partisans of Corday being sharpened, ready to assassinate the patriots.
Archives Nationales, F7 4774 29 d2.

The armée révolutionnaire at Lyon

On 12 October 1793 the Convention decreed the destruction of the rebel city of Lyon and the setting up of a memorial with the inscription 'Lyon made war on liberty, Lyon no longer exists'. The remaining buildings were to be called 'Commune-Affranchie'. Ronsin's letter tells of the role of the 'armée révolutionnaire' of Paris in the conquest of Lyon.

The General-in-Chief of the Revolutionary Army, to his brothers and friends the Cordeliers. The Revolutionary Army on 5 Frimaire (25 November 1793) entered that guilty city, so wrongly called Commune Affranchie. Terror was painted on every brow; and the complete silence that I had taken care to impose on our brave soldiers, made their march even more menacing, more terrible; most of the shops were closed: some women stood alongside our route; one read in their eyes more indignation than fear. The men remained hidden in their dens from which they had sallied forth, during the siege, only to assassinate the true friends of liberty.

The guillotine and the firing squad did justice to more than four hundred rebels. But a new revolutionary commission has just been established, consisting of true sans-culottes: my colleague Parein is its president, and in a few days the grape shot, fired by our cannoneers, will have delivered to us, in one single moment, more than four thousand conspirators. It is time to cut down the procedure! delay can awaken, I will not say courage, but the despair of traitors who are still hidden among the debris of that impious town. The Republic has need of a great example − the Rhône, reddened with blood, must carry to its banks and to the sea, the corpses of those cowards who murdered our brothers; and whilst the thunderbolt, which must exterminate them in an instant, will carry terror into the departments where the seed of rebellion was sown, it is necessary that the flames from their devastated dens proclaim far and wide the punishment that is destined for those who try to imitate them.

These measures are all the more urgent because, in that commune of one hundred and twenty thousand inhabitants, you would scarcely find, I shall not say fifteen hundred patriots, but fifteen hundred men who had not been accomplices of the rebellion; but thanks to the representatives of the people and to the Jacobins, sent into the commune, the vigilance of the constituted authorities everywhere pursues suspect persons and paralyses, as it were, with fear, the great number of those who secretly aspire only to plunge their knives into us. Already the cowards have assassinated one of our revolutionary soldiers during the night; decide, then, brothers and friends, if it is not time to use the most prompt and most terrible means of justice! this great event is being prepared, and we hope that, before the end of Frimaire, all the authors and accomplices of the rebellion will have paid for their crimes.

Salut et fraternité.   RONSIN

Les Révolutions de Paris, no. 218, 18-27 Frimaire, Year II (8-17 Dec. 1793). Translation from J. Gilchrest and W.J. Murray, *The Press in the French Revolution,* Cheshire and Ginn, 1971, pp. 287-8.

The armée révolutionnaire at Pontoise

*This report by a detachment of the Parisian 'armée révolution-
naire' to the general assembly of the Section of the Observatory
on 16 March 1794 shows the day-to-day work of provisioning
the cities, especially Paris.*

Liberty, Equality, Fraternity or Death. The Revolutionary
Army at Pontoise sur l'Oise, north west of Paris. Citizens
and Brothers. The citizen soldiers of the Revolutionary Army,
still imbued with Revolutionary principles, are now stationed
at Pontoise and assure you that they have only left Paris and
their homes to thwart Intrigue and Aristocracy to the utmost.
From the moment we arrived here, we have been occupied in
arranging the provisioning of Paris. Several of our comrades,
in the course of their duties, have found eggs and butter
hidden in cupboards in farmhouses and even grain hidden
in barrels.

The very mention of our name makes traitors go pale.
For more than three months we have demanded the authority
to exercise full surveillance. Our demands have been in vain.
Our brother citizens lack everything, and if we do not have
sufficient food, it is because the scarcity is only apparent.
We ask that we might search households, which we have not
done so far, at least only feebly. We ask that the Revolutionary
Commissioners send us a true *Sans Culotte,* authorised to
override the authority of the local Commune. By such means
we shall foil the counter-revolutionaries who go into the
countryside and buy up foodstuffs in order to sell them to
the rich and selfish at inflated prices.

We ask that we be allowed to requisition food and bring it
to Paris. We made such a demand to the Commission for
Provisioning the Republic, but have had no reply. Now
calumny directs its steps towards us; that is why we ask you
to give us the chance to prove that we are still Republicans
and supporters of the Mountain. We are obliged to tell you
that it is the incompetence of the municipal authorities that
is the sole cause of the shortage of basic necessities.

Archives Nationales, W159.

A justification of the Terror

This speech by Saint-Just on 26 February 1794 was occasioned by demands from the Convention that reports be made on the thousands of political prisoners awaiting trial. The so-called Indulgents tended to believe in the innocence of many of these prisoners and Saint-Just struck back at them.

Citizens, how could anyone delude himself that you are inhuman? Your Revolutionary Tribunal has condemned three hundred rogues to death within a year. Has not the Spanish Inquisition done worse than that, and, my God, for what a cause! Have the assizes in England slaughtered no one in that period? And what about Bender, who roasts Belgian babies? What of the dungeons of Germany, where people are entombed, do you ever hear about them? What about the kings of Europe, does anyone moan to them about pity? Oh, do not allow yourselves to become soft-hearted! ...
To see the indulgence that is advocated by a few, you would think that they were the masters of our own destiny and the chief priests of freedom. Since the month of May last, our history is a lesson about the terrible extremities to which indulgence leads. In that period, Dumouriez had abandoned our conquests; patriots were being assassinated in Frankfort; Custine had abandoned Mainz, the Palatinate and the banks of the Rhine; Calvados was in revolt; the Vendée was victorious; Lyon, Bordeaux, Marseille and Toulon were in arms against the French people; Condé, Valenciennes and Le Quesnoy had capitulated; our armies were being beaten in the Pyrenees and around Mont Blanc. you were being betrayed by everyone and it seemed as if men headed the government and the armies only to destroy them and plunder the debris. The navy was bribed, the arsenals and ships were in ashes; the currency was undermined, our banks and industries were controlled by foreigners. Yet the greatest of our misfortunes was a certain fear of the concentration of authority necessary to save the state. The conspirators of the party of the Right had blunted in advance, by an unsuspected stratagem, the weapons which you might later use to resist and punish them ... today there

are still some who would like once again to break these weapons.

C. Vellay, ed., *Oeuvres Complètes de Saint-Just,* Paris, 1908, ii, 236-7.

document 19

The crime of indifference

Many people tried by Revolutionary tribunals under the Terror were accused of indifference, under Article 10 of the Law of Suspects of 10 September 1793. Among those charged with doing nothing to advance the Revolutionary cause was Jean Sellon, a lawyer who appeared before the Marseille tribunal. Indifference was regarded as a more serious offence for a man of means and education.

He possesses a very moderate patriotism. If he can give proof of civic responsibility, it is only by acts which are common to many people. He has never wished to take a firmly committed attitude. If he has never frequently attended the sectional assembly, it is rather out of fear of compromising himself than of wishing to serve the public good. He has allowed his knowledge and enlightenment to flounder in the greatest danger of purposeless liberty. He cannot say that he has openly condemned the counter-revolution.

Archives départementales, Bouches-du-Rhône, L3118, 27 Germinal, an II (16 April 1794).

document 20

Infamous words

Some of the charges under the Law of Suspects verged on the ridiculous, though taken very seriously. At Limoges, the Revolutionary tribunal called in expert opinion in the form of two writing masters to decide upon the guilt of a volunteer, Gabriel David. The experts decided that the 'mots infâmes' on the leave pass were in his hand and he was found guilty and imprisoned.

There was tried before us, in accordance with the indictment, Gabriel David, who was interrogated as follows:

Did you write 'Shit on the nation' on your leave pass?

He replied 'No'; that he did not know how the shocking words got there and did not know whose was the sacrilegious hand which had written them; that he had been taken by surprise when the commissioner for war had read them to him, that he swore once again that he was not the author and as evidence of his innocence pointed to the fact that if his leave pass had contained anything counter-revolutionary he would have consigned it to the flames rather than have shown it to the commissioner for war.

Archives départementales, Haute-Vienne, L843, 28 Messidor an II (16 July 1794).

document 21

The popularity of Robespierre

This extract from the deliberations of the 'comité de surveil-lance' of Libourne on 14 November 1793 is from a list recom-mending the arrest of certain people and sending them before the military commission in Bordeaux. Criticism of Robespierre is equated with 'incivisme', federalism and hoarding.

Citizen Dumas senior, the ex-Constituent, a suspect because of his indifference, his sordid avarice, and his hatred of public assemblies, always holding himself aloof and never having shown any sign of patriotism; and for having shown, when he was in the Constituent Assembly, a marked hatred of the republican Robespierre, writing to one of his cousins, who lives in this town, that he never wished to defile his pen with the name of Robespierre.

Archives Gironde, 13 L49, cited by R.C. Cobb in *Annales Historiques de la Révolution Française,* vol. xxxvii, 1965, p. 491.

document 22

Apathy in lower Normandy

This extract is from a report by Citizen Le Grand, on a mission to Normandy as an agent of the government in July 1793, especially concerned with finding supplies of food for Paris,

at a time when the federalist revolt in Caen was at its zenith.
He is writing to the Ministry of the Interior.

In the area of the Auge, as in all the part of Calvados on this side of Caen, the inhabitants seem thoroughly apathetic towards the Revolution, and regard it with more curiosity than interest. One gathers from their talk that they are exhausted by the excessive increases in the price of basic necessities and,. even more so, by the rarity and poor quality of bread; they have no clear opinions about anything else, they await events and pray for the restoration of order and calm. The towns of Pont l'Evêque and Honfleur, the only ones there are in these parts, share the same outlook and, up till now, have done nothing to raise levies of men...
Pont l'Evêque, 27 July 1793, 2nd year of the Republic. Archives Nationales, F20 170, cited by J.M. Lévy, AHRF, vol. xxxv, 1963, p. 225.

document 23

The principles of Revolutionary government

This speech, delivered by Robespierre on 25 December 1793, argued that France had not yet reached the stage where peaceful constitutional government was possible. Until France had conquered her enemies, there had to be Revolutionary government and a more severe policy of intimidation, including a speedier and more efficient Revolutionary Tribunal.

The theory of Revolutionary government is as new as the Revolution which has developed it ... the function of government is to direct the moral and physical resources of the nation towards its essential aim. The aim of constitutional government is to preserve the Republic: that of Revolutionary government is to put the Republic on a secure foundation. The Revolution is the war of liberty against its enemies; the constitution is the régime of victorious and peace-loving liberty. Revolutionary government needs to be extraordinarily active, precisely because it is at war. It is subject to less uniform and rigorous rules, because the circumstances in which it finds itself are tempestuous and changing, and above all because it is obliged to employ ceaselessly new and urgent resources for new and pressing threats.

Constitutional government is primarily concerned with civil liberty: revolutionary government with public liberty. Under a constitutional régime it is more or less enough to protect individuals against abuses of government. Under a revolutionary régime the government itself is obliged to defend itself against all the factions which threaten it. Revolutionary government gives public protection to good citizens: to the enemies of the people it deals out only death. ...

If revolutionary government has to be more active in its policies and more free in its actions than ordinary government, is it then less just and less legitimate? No: it rests on the most sacred of all laws, the safety of the people; and on the most irrefutable of all arguments: that of necessity. Revolutionary government has rules of its own, resting on the principles of justice and public order. It has no room for anarchy and disorder; its aim, on the contrary, is to repress them, in order to affirm and develop the rule of law; it has no time for the arbitrary. It is not directed by individual feelings, but by the public interest...It is necessary to navigate between two rocks: weakness and boldness, reaction and extremism...

Archives Parlémentaires, vol. lxxxii, Paris 1913, p. 300.

document 24

The Republic of Virtue

Robespierre's speech of 5 February 1794 set down the moral aims of the Revolution. Revolutionary terror would lead to a new republic of virtue, where everyone would respect the nation and its laws and the sovereignty of the people.

What is our ultimate aim? The peaceful enjoyment of liberty and equality; the reign of eternal justice, whose laws are engraved, not on marble or stone, but in the hearts of all men, even in that of the slave who forgets them and of the tyrant who rejects them. *(Applause)* We desire to see an order of things where all base and cruel feelings are suppressed, and where the law encourages beneficent and generous feelings; where ambition means the desire for glory and the service of the Republic; where social distinctions emerge from conditions of equality; where the citizen is subject to the magistrate, the magistrate to the people, and the people to the principle of justice; where the nation assures the well-being of every individual and where every individual proudly enjoys the prosperity and glory of the nation; where all men's spirits are uplifted by the continual sharing of republican sentiments, and by the need to be worthy of the esteem of a great people, where the arts adorn the liberty which ennobles them; where commerce is a source of public wealth, not only of the monstrous affluence of a few families. In our country we wish to substitute morality for egoism, honesty for mere love of honour, principles for customs, duties for convention, the reign of reason for the tyranny of fashion, the fear of vice for the fear of bad luck; we want to substitute pride for insolence, magnanimity for vanity, love of glory for love of money, good men for mere good company, merit for intrigue, genius for slickness, truth for brilliance, the appeal of happiness for the boredom of sensuality, the grandeur of man for the pettiness of great men; a happy, powerful and magnanimous people for one that is amiable, frivolous and discontented. That is to say, we wish to replace the vices and follies of monarchy by the virtues and miraculous achievements of the Republic. *(Applause)* In a word, we wish to fulfil the plan of nature and promote the destiny of humanity, to fulfil the promises of enlightened philosophy, to absolve providence for a long reign of crime and tyranny. All this in order that France, formerly illustrious among enslaved countries, will eclipse the glory of all the free peoples who have ever existed and will become a model for all nations to imitate; so that France will become the scourge of oppressors, the saviour of the oppressed, the bright star of the universe; and whilst we seal our achievements with our blood, we can at least see the stars of universal happiness shining ... that is our ambition: that is our aim.

Archives Parlémentaires, vol. lxxxiv, Paris 1962, p. 143.

document 25

Revolutionary enthusiasm

This address, sent by the 'société populaire' of Bergerac, in the Dordogne, to the National Convention on 16 April 1794 after the arrest and execution of the Dantonists, provides an insight into the attitudes and activities of local militants, with their somewhat inflated sense of importance.

Legislators — We shook with indignation when we learned that you have been surrounded by the darkest conspiracy. What! Were they trying to destroy the national government? It would have been the most pure and zealous defenders of the people who would have been the first victims! The Mountain has been polluted by conspirators! The monsters! They have suffered the fate of enemies of the nation. Your courage and determined surveillance will continue to strike such blows...

Destroy all factions with the same energy, annihilate all plots aiming to undermine liberty. Our Parisian brothers are there already. They will preserve the integrity of the national government. Foreigners, traitors in disguise, still circulate among them...

If they need assistance, we demand to be the first to be called and, as at the time of the overthrow of the monarchy, we will be the first to arrive. We see saltpetre piling up abundantly before our eyes. An arms factory which, without fear of contradiction, will be one of the most important in the Republic, is rising within our walls as if by magic. Already a vast quantity of excellent lock-plates [for firearms] has been manufactured. Lakanal, your worthy colleague [commissaire in the Dordogne], gave it its initial revolutionary impetus. That he would soon return among us to give it the finishing touch! His presence is necessary here; it is required by the national interest and by our wishes. Here fanaticism and superstition have given way to reason. It is in the Temple of Reason that, each revolutionary week, we learn to seal the knot of fraternity and patriotism. We have never forced priests to renounce their vocation. They realised that their reign was over and shut up shop at once.

Printed in H. Labroue, *La Société Populaire de Bergerac pendant la Révolution,* Paris, Librairie Rieder, 1915, p. 356

Glossary

ancien régime, term invented in the 1790s for the way of life and government in France destroyed by the Revolution in 1789

armées révolutionnaires, civilian 'armies' operating in France whose primary tasks were to requisition grain and enforce political orthodoxy in the Year II

bourgeois, carried a variety of meanings in the eighteenth century; used loosely in this book to mean the propertied classes below the nobility and above the peasants and urban workers

cahiers (de doléances), lists of grievances drawn up by each of the three estates or orders at the time of elections for the States-General in 1789

certificat de civisme, document attesting to the political orthodoxy of the holder; a kind of 'Revolutionary passport'

comités de surveillance, police committees elected by the assemblies of the sections; they tended to assume wide powers of local government

fédérés, contingents of armed men sent in 1792 from the provinces to Paris, in order to defend the capital against attack from the northeast frontier

menu peuple ('little people'), the common people

journées, the great Revolutionary 'Days', such as 14 July 1789 or 10 August 1793, involving popular insurrection

parlements, thirteen law courts which exercised judicial powers and the right to register royal decrees; saw themselves as a (non-elected) brake on 'absolutism'

'Père Duchesne', Hébert's scurrilous, vitriolic and obscene newspaper; the favourite reading of the *sans culottes;* applied also as his nickname, for the paper was ostensibly the words of an irascible *sans culotte,* often identified with Hébert himself.

problème des subsistances, the vexed question of provisioning urban markets

représentants en mission, members of the Convention sent to the provinces and the armies in 1793 with full administrative powers

sections, wards of the electoral districts of urban communes; transformed by the *sans culottes* into powerful political units

taxation populaire, price control by crowd action, usually involving the seizure and sale of goods at a 'fair' price

Chronological Summary

1786	August	Calonne's land tax proposals
1787	February	Assembly of the Notables
	May	Brienne succeeded Calonne; dismissal of the Notables
1788	May-July	Suspension of the Parlements; 'revolt of the nobility'
	Aug-Sept	Brienne succeeded by Necker; Parlements recalled
1789	April	Riots in Paris and the provinces
	May	States-General met
	June	Tennis Court Oath: Royal Session
	July	Dismissal of Necker; fall of the Bastille; the 'Great Fear'
	August	Abolition of feudal rights; Declaration of Rights
	September	Defeat of the '*monarchiens*'
	October	March to Versailles
	November	Decrees on the Church, local government and *assignats*
1790	Feb-Mar	Religious conflict in Nîmes
	June	Abolition of the nobility
	July	Civil Constitution of the Clergy
	November	Enforcement of the clerical oath
1791	June	Flight to Varennes
	July	Massacre on the Champ de Mars
	August	Declaration of Pillnitz
	September	King accepted the Constitution and the Constituent Assembly dissolved
	October	Meeting of the Legislative Assembly
1792	April	Declaration of war with Austria
	June	First invasion of the Tuileries
	July	Brunswick Manifesto and agitation in the Paris sections
	August	Revolution of 10 August and suspension of the king; Beginning of the 'First Terror'

	September	Fall of Verdun; September Massacres; Battle of Valmy; meeting of the Convention; abolition of the monarchy and beginning of the Year I of the Republic
	November	Battle of Jemappes; French armies into Belgium
	December	Trial of the king
1793	January	Execution of Louis XVI
	February	War with England; food riots in Paris; the *enragés*
	March	War with Spain; outbreak of revolt in La Vendée
	April	Establishment of the Committee of Public Safety; first *maximum* (grain)
	May	Federalist revolts at Lyon, Marseille, Caen and Bordeaux
	June	Fall of the Girondins; Jacobin Constitution of 1793
	July	Robespierre entered the Committee of Public Safety
	August	*Levée en masse*; surrender of Toulon to the English
	September	Beginning of Year II of the Republic; Terror 'the order of the day'; law of suspects; general *maximum;* creation of the Parisian *armée revolutionnaire*
	October	Government declared 'Revolutionary until the peace'; recapture of Lyon by Republican forces; trial and execution of the Girondins
	November	Festival of Reason
	December	Reorganisation of Revolutionary Government by the law of 14 frimaire; defeat of the Vendée rebels; English evacuated Toulon
1794	February	Laws of Ventôse
	March	Arrest of the 'Hébertists' and 'Dantonists'
	May	Attempts to assassinate Robespierre
	June	Festival of the Supreme Being
	July	Maximum wage legislation; arrest and execution of Robespierre and his followers
	November	Jacobin Club closed
	December	Abolition of the *maximum*
1795	April	Rising of Germinal
	May	Rising of Prairial
	August	Constitution of the Year III
	October	Rising of Vendémiaire; dissolution of the Convention and the beginning of the Directory

Bibliography

The literature on the French Revolution is immense and what follows is necessarily a personal and therefore partial selection, with some bias towards fairly readily available works in English.

DOCUMENTS: While there are massive French collections of documentary material, relatively few of them are available to English readers outside a few major libraries. The following may be consulted (texts are in French unless otherwise stated).

1   Thompson, J.M. *French Revolution Documents 1789-94.* Blackwell 1933.
2   Roberts, J.M. *French Revolution Documents, i,* (1787 to 10 August 1792) Blackwell 1966. *Vol. ii, ed. J. Hardman,* 1974.
3   Stewart, J.H. *A Documentary Survey of the French Revolution,* Macmillan, New York, 1951. Documents in English
4   Gershoy, L. *The Era of the French Revolution 1789-99,* Anvil Books 1958 has a useful documentary section in English.
5   Markov, W. and Soboul, A. *Die Sansculotten von Paris,* Akademie-Verlag E. Berlin 1957, prints documents in French and German parallel texts.
6   Gilchrest, J. and Murray, W.T. *The Press in the French Revolution,* Ginn 1971, translates extracts from the Paris press between 1789 and 1794.

The French Revolution is placed in its European context by:

7   Lefebvre, G. 'La Révolution Française dans l'histoire du monde', *Annales,* 1948.
8   Brinton, C.C. *A Decade of Revolution 1789-99,* New York, Harper, 1934.
9   Rudé, G. *Revolutionary Europe 1783-1815,* Fontana, 1964.
10 Rudé, G. *Europe in the Eighteenth Century,* Weidenfeld & Nicolson, 1972.
11 Ford, F.L. *Europe 1780-1830,* Longman, 1970.
12 Hobsbawm, E.J. *The Age of Revolution 1789-1848,* Weidenfeld and Nicolson, 1962; Mentor paperback.
13 Goodwin, A., ed. *The American and French Revolutions 1763-93,* vol. viii of the New Cambridge Modern History, Cambridge University Press, 1965, editor's introduction.

Two books which argue the thesis of the 'Atlantic Revolution' are:

14 Palmer, R.R. *The Age of the Democratic Revolution,* vol. i, *The Challenge;* vol. ii, *The Struggle,* Princeton University Press, 1959, 1964 (paperback 1969).

15 Godechot, J. *Les Révolutions 1770-1799,* 'Nouvelle Clio', 36, Paris, P.U.F., 1963, which contains a valuable bibliography of secondary works and a guide to primary sources. The narrative sections have been translated as *France and the Atlantic Revolution of the Eighteenth Century,* New York, Collier-Macmillan, 1971.

See also:

16 Palmer, R.R. 'The world revolution of the West: 1763-1801', *Political Science Quarterly,* lxiv, 1954, and Amann, P. ed. *The Eighteenth-Century Revolution: French or Western,* Heath/Harrap 1963, and Cobban, A. 'The age of the democratic Revolution', *History,* clv, 1960.

For good introductory surveys of the French Revolution see:

17 Goodwin, A. *The French Revolution,* Hutchinson University Library, 1953. The best short book on the Revolution.

18 Hampson, N. *A Social History of the French Revolution,* Routledge, 1963; paperback 1966. Especially good on changes in the social structure and the role of the provinces.

19 Sydenham, M.J. *The French Revolution,* Batsford 1965; University paperback, 1969. A lucid narrative which concentrates on the years 1791-94 from the traditional point of view of Paris and political conflicts.

20 Soboul, A. *Précis d'Histoire de la Révolution Française, Paris,* Éditions Sociales, 1962. A supple Marxist interpretation.

21 Cobban, A. *A History of Modern France,* vol. i, Penguin, 1957.

Among larger studies of the Revolution are:

22 Lefebvre, G. *La Révolution française,* 'Peuples et Civilisations, xiii' Paris, P.U.F., 6th ed, 1968. The outstanding book on the Revolutionary period. There is an indifferent English translation in two volumes: *The French Revolution from its Origins to 1793; The French Revolution from 1793-1799,* Routledge 1962, 1964.

23 Mathiez, A. *La Révolution Française,* Paris, Leclerc, 1922-27; English translation; *The French Revolution,* New York, Russell 1962.

24 Thompson, J.M. *The French Revolution,* Blackwell, 1943.

25 Furet, F. and Richet, D. *La Révolution,* Paris, Hachette, 1965; English translation; *The French Revolution,* Weidenfeld & Nicolson, 1970.

A splendid essay, which emphasizes the history of ideas and contains superb illustrations, is:

26   Hampson, N. *The First European Revolution 1776-1815*, Thames & Hudson 1969.

For the historiography of the Revolution see **15**, *part iii*, **39**, *introduction, and:*

27   Geyl, P. *Encounters in History,* Fontana, 1967, part ii, ch 2.
28   Cobban, A. *Historians and the Causes of the French Revolution,* Historical Association pamphlet, G.2, 1958.
29   Cobban, A. introductory essay in his *Aspects of the French Revolution,* Cape 1968, Paladin paperback 1971, where **28** is reprinted.
30   Rudé, G. *Interpretations of the French Revolution,* Historical Association pamphlet, G.47, 1961.
31   McManners, J. 'The historiography of the French Revolution', ch. xxii in **13**.
32   Goodwin, A. 'The recent historiography of the French Revolution' in Moody, T.W. ed. *Historical Studies VI,* Routledge, 1968; see also: Friguglietti, J. 'Albert Mathiez: an historian at war', *French Historical Studies,* vii, 4, 1972.

For recent criticisms of the French Jacobin-Marxist school, which views the Revolution as a class struggle and the victory of the bourgeosie over 'feudalism', see:

33   Cobban, A. *The Social Interpretation of the French Revolution,* Cambridge University Press. 1964, paperback 1968.
34   Behrens, B. 'Professor Cobban and his critic', *Historical Journal,* ix, 1966.
35   Behrens, B. ' "Straight history" and "History in depth" ', *Historical Journal,* vii, 1965.
36   Taylor, G.V. 'Types of capitalism in eighteenth-century France', *English Historical Review,* 1964.
37   Taylor, G.V. 'Noncapitalist wealth and the origins of the French Revolution', *American Historical Review,* lxxii, 1967.
38   Kaplow, J., Shapiro, G. and Eisenstein, E.L. 'Class in the French Revolution', *American Historical Review,* lxxii, 1967; see also: Palmer, R.R. 'Sur le rôle de la bourgeoisie dans la Révolution française', *Annales Historiques de la Révolution Française* [AHRF], 1967
39   Kaplow, J., ed. *New Perspectives on the French Revolution,*

Wiley, 1965: a collection of translated articles (minus footnotes) by distinguished scholars on French social structure, the outbreak of the Revolution, popular movements and 'collective mentalities'.

40   Lewis, G. *Life in Revolutionary France,* Batsford/Putnam 1972 is a shrewd survey, well illustrated, of how the Revolution affected the people, especially the *classes populaires.*

There is a wealth of learned monographs and articles on the 'ancien régime' in France, but a shortage of up-to-date general works. See:

41   Behrens, C.B.A. *The Ancien Régime,* Thames & Hudson 1967, the best survey in English, magnificently illustrated.

42   Sagnac, P. *La Formation de la Société Française Moderne,* vol. ii, Paris, P.U.F., 1946 is the standard work.

43   Méthivier, M. *L'Ancien Régime,* Paris, P.U.F., 1961, in the brief *'Que Sais-je?'* series.

44   Sagnac, P. 'La crise de l'économie française à la fin de l'Ancien Régime et au début de la Révolution', *Revue d'Histoire Economique et Sociale,* iii, 1950.

45   McManners, J. 'France', ch. 2 in Goodwin, A., ed. *The European Nobility in the Eighteenth Century,* A. and C. Black, 1953.

46   Dakin, D. 'The breakdown of the old regime in France', ch. xxi in **13**.

Among a vast number of local studies are:

47   Lefebvre, G. 'Urban society in the Orléanais in the eighteenth century', *Past and Present,* xix, 1961.

48   Forster, R. *The Nobility of Toulouse in the Eighteenth Century,* Oxford University Press, 1960.

49   Godechot, J. and Moncassin, S. 'Les structures sociales de Toulouse en 1749 et en 1785', *AHRF,* 1965.

50   Kaplow, J. *Elbeuf During the Revolutionary Period: history and social structure,* Johns Hopkins University Press, 1964.

51   Hufton, O.H. *Bayeux in the Late Eighteenth Century,* Oxford University Press, 1967. (See also no. **93** below for Southern Anjou and **94** for the Sarthe)

For the 'pre-revolution' of 1787-89 see **41** *above, ch. 4, and:*

52   Lefebvre, G. *The Coming of the French Revolution,* Princeton University Press, 1947, translation by R.R. Palmer of *Quatre-Vingt-Neuf,* Paris, 1939. A beautiful little book.

53 Egret, J. *La Pre-Révolution Française 1787-1788,* Paris, P.U.F., 1962.
54 Egret, J. 'Les origines de la Révolution en Bretagne 1788-1789', *Revue Historique,* ccxiii, 1955.
55 Egret, J. 'La pré-révolution en Provence 1787-1789, *AHRF,* 1954. Both M. Egret's articles are translated in **39,** as are:
56 Lemoigne, Y. 'Population and provisions in Strasbourg in the eighteenth century', and:
57 Trénard, L. 'The social crisis in Lyons on the eve of the French Revolution'.
58 Goodwin, A. 'Calonne, the Assembly of the French Notables of 1787 and the origins of the *Révolte Nobilaire', English Historical Review,* lxi, 1946.
59 Rudé, G. 'The outbreak of the French Revolution', *Past and Present,* viii, 1955.
60 Greenlaw, R.W. 'Pamphlet literature in France during the period of the aristocratic revolt (1787-88)', *Journal of Modern History,* xxi, 1957.
61 Doyle, W. 'The Parlements of France and the breakdown of the old regime', *French Historical Studies,* vi, 1970.

There is a substantial literature on the impact of the French enlighten-ment. See **26** *and:*
62 Hampson, N. *The Enlightenment,* Penguin, 1968: lucid, elegant and original.
63 Cobban, A. 'The Enlightenment and the French Revolution', in **29.**
64 Macdonald, J. *Rousseau and the French Revolution 1762-1791,* Athlone Press, 1965.
65 Richet, D. 'Autour des origines idéologiques lointaines de la Révolution francaise', *Annales,* 1969.
66 Ford, F.L. 'The Revolutionary-Napoleonic period: how much of a watershed?', *American Historical Review,* lxix, 1963.
67 Doyle, W. 'Was there an aristocratic reaction in pre-Revolutionary France?', *Past and Present,* lvii, 1972.
68 Davies, A. 'The origins of the French Peasant Revolution of 1789', *History,* xlix, 1964.
69 Greenlaw, R.W., ed. *Economic Origins of the French Revolution: poverty or prosperity?,* Heath/Harrap, 1958.
70 De Tocqueville, Alexis. *The Ancien Régime and the French Revolution,* English translation: Fontana, 1966. One of the world's great masterpieces of historical interpretation.

For popular movements from 1775 and the importance of bread prices see:
71 Rudé, G., *The Crowd in the French Revolution,* Oxford University Press, 1959.
72 Rudé, G., *Paris and London in the Eighteenth Century,* Fontana, 1970, a collection of learned articles.
73 Lefebvre, G. 'Le mouvement des prix et les origines de la Révolution française', *AHRF,* 1937.

For the events of 1789 prior to 14 July see 52 and 59 above and:
74 Godechot, J. *La Prise de la Bastille,* Paris, Gallimard, 1965; English translation: *The Taking of the Bastille,* Faber, 1970.
75 Lefebvre, G. 'Foules révolutionnaires', *AHRF,* 1934, translation in **39**.
76 Egret, J. *La Révolution des Notables: Mounier et les Monarchiens,* Paris, Armand Colin, 1950.
77 Hutt, M.G. 'The role of the curés in the Estates General of 1789', *Journal of Ecclesiastical History,* vi, 1955.
78 Rudé, G. 'The Fall of the Bastille', *History Today,* iv, 1954, reprinted in **72**.
79 Lefebvre, G. 'La Révolution Française et les paysans', *AHRF,* 1933.
80 Rudé, G. 'La composition sociale des insurrections parisiennes de 1789 à 1791', *AHRF,* 1952, trans. in **72**.

On the peasant insurrection, the 'Great Fear' and the municipal revolution see 52, ch. 10, and:
81 Lefebvre, G. *La Grande Peur de 1789,* Paris, SÉDÉS, 1932; English translation: *The Great Fear of 1789,* New Left Books Ltd, 1973.
82 Ligou, D. 'A propos de la Révolution Municipale', *Revue d'Histoire Économique et Sociale,* xxxviii, 1960.

For the political conflicts of August and September 1789 and the October Days see above 76 and 52, ch. 10, and:
83 Bradby, E.D. *Barnave,* Oxford University Press, 1915, 2 vols.
84 Mathiez, A. 'Étude critique sur les journées des 5 et 6 octobre 1789', *Revue Historique, lxvii, 1898.*

On the Church, see:
85 McManners, J. *The French Revolution and the Church,* SPCK paperback, 1969: brief and beautifully written.

On the work of the Constituent Assembly and the rivalries in the Legislative Assembly, see:

86   Thompson, E. *Popular Sovereignty and the French Constituent Assembly,* Manchester University Press, 1952.
87   Poperen, J. and Lefebvre, G. 'Études sur le ministère de Narbonne', *AHRF,* 1947.
88   Michon, G. *Essai sur l'Histoire du Parti Feuillant: Adrien Duport,* Paris, Puyot, 1924.
89   Brinton, C.C. *The Jacobins,* 1930, New York, Russell, 1961.

For the counter-revolution and the origins of the war, see:

90   Godechot, J. *The Counter-Revolution 1789-1804,* Routledge, 1972.
91   Biro, S.G. *The German Policy of Revolutionary France,* Harvard University Press, 1957.
92   Hood, J.N. 'Protestant and Catholic relations and the roots of the first popular counter-revolutionary movement in France', *Journal of Modern History,* xlii, 1971.
93   Tilly, C. *The Vendée,* Harvard University Press, Arnold 1964.
94   Bois, P. *Les Paysans de l'Ouest,* Le Mans, Vilaire, 1960.
95   Chaumié, J., *Le Réseau d'Antraigues et la Contre-Révolution 1791-93,* Paris, Gallimard, 1965.

For the flight to Varennes, the Champ de Mars and the fall of the monarchy, see **71**, *chs 6 and 7;* **22**, *book iii, ch 3, and:*

96   Reinhard, M. *La Chute de la Royauté: 10 Août 1792,* Paris, Gallimard, 1969. Now the standard work.
97   Reinhard, M. *Nouvelle histoire de Paris: la Révolution,* Paris, Hachette, 1972.
98   Vovelle, M. *La Chute de la Monarchie 1787-92,* Paris, Seuil, 1972: a stimulating view from the Midi and the south-east.
99   Sydenham, M. *The Girondins,* Athlone Press, 1961: challenges the view of Mathiez that the Girondins were a coherent social group. See also:
100   Patrick, A. 'Political divisions in the French National Convention 1792-93', *Journal of Modern History,* xli, 1969.
101   Sydenham, M.J. 'The Montagnards and their opponents', *ibid,* xliii, 1971.

On the 'sans culottes' see **5** *(documents),* **40**, *ch. 5, and:*

102   Soboul, A. *The Parisian Sans-Culottes and the French Revolution,* Oxford University Press, 1964, a translation of the second part

of Soboul's mighty thesis *Les Sans-culottes Parisiens en l'an II*, Paris, Clavreuil, 1958, which constitutes a landmark in Revolutionary studies.

103 Soboul, A. *Paysans, Sans-culottes et Jacobins,* Paris, Clavreuil, 1965: a stimulating collection of articles.

104 Cobb, R.C., *Les Armées Révolutionnaires: instrument de la Terreur dans les départements,* 2 vols. Paris, Mouton, and The Hague 1961-63: a massive and seminal work on the Terror in the departments which throws a good deal of light on *sans-culotte* attitudes.

105 Cobb, R.C. *Terreur et Subsistances,* Paris, Clavreuil, 1965: a collection of articles on the provincial Terror in Years II and III.

106 Cobb, R.C. *The Police and the People: French Popular Protest 1789-1820,* Oxford University Press, 1970; paperback, 1972: a dazzling view of the Revolution from the very bottom of society.

107 Williams, G.A. *Artisans and Sans Culottes,* Arnold 1968: a brief, buoyant and staccato comparison of English and French popular movements. An exciting book.

108 Cobb, R.C. 'The revolutionary mentality in France 1793-94', *History,* xlii, 1957. See also his 'Quelques aspects de la mentalité révolutionnaire', reprinted in **105**.

109 Hufton, O. 'The life of the very poor in the eighteenth century' in Cobban, A., ed. *The Eighteenth Century,* Thames & Hudson 1969.

For the 'First Terror' and the September Massacres, see:
110 Caron, P. *La Première Terreur,* Paris, P.U.F., 1950.

111 Caron, P., *Les Massacres de Septembre,* Paris, Maison du Livre Française, 1935.

On the crisis of February-June 1793, see above **71, 99, 93,** and:
112 Mathiez, A. *La Vie Chère et Le Mouvement Social sous la Terreur,* Paris, Armand Colin, 1927.

113 Rudé, G. 'Les Émeutes des 25, 26 février 1793', *AHRF,* 1960.

114 Markov, W. 'Les Jacquesroutins', *AHRF,* 1960, on the *enragés.*

115 Rose, R.B. *The Enragés: Socialists of the French Revolution?,* Melbourne University Press, 1965.

116 Cobb, R.C. *A Second Identity,* Oxford University Press, 1969: see essays 6 and 10 for the *enragés* and the Vendée.

117 Hufton, O. 'Women in Revolution 1780-96', *Past and Present,* liii, 1971: a pioneering and compassionate article.

118 Tilly, C. 'Local conflicts in the Vendée before the rebellion of 1793', *French Historical Studies,* ii, 1961.

119 Tilly, C. 'The analysis of a counter-revolution', *History and Theory,* iii, 1963.

120 Walter, G. *La Guerre de Vendée,* Paris, Plon, 1953.

121 Goodwin, A. 'Counter-revolution in Brittany', *Bulletin of the John Rylands Library, Manchester,* xxxix, 1957.

122 Goodwin, A. 'The Federalist Movement in Caen during the French Revolution', *ibid,* xlii, 1960.

123 Balzac, Honoré de, *The Chouans,* trans. Penguin 1972, is an exciting and revealing novel about counter-revolution in Brittany; set in 1799 and written in 1825-29.

There is a large and rapidly growing literature on the Terror of 1793-94. See **104-107** *and:*

124 Bouloiseau, M. *La République jacobine: 10 août 1792-9 thermidor an II,* Paris, Seuil, 1972.

125 Walter, G. *Histoire de la Terreur 1793-1794,* Paris, Albin Michel, 1937.

126 Greer, D. *The Incidence of the Terror in the French Revolution,* Harvard University Press, 1935.

127 Palmer, R.R., *Twelve Who Ruled,* Princeton University Press, 1941; paperback, 1970, on the Committee of Public Safety.

128 Bouloiseau, M. *Le Comité de salut public,* new edn, 'Que Sais-je?', Paris, P.U.F., 1968.

129 Cobb, R.C. *Reactions to the French Revolution,* Oxford University Press, 1972: a brilliant study of the counter-revolutionary and criminal classes.

130 Lucas, C. *The Structure of the Terror,* Oxford University Press, 1973: a study of the department of the Loire.

131 Scott, W. *Terror and Repression in Revolutionary Marseilles,* Macmillan, 1973; a fine study of the fear and ruthlessness engendered by the Revolution in 1793.

132 Cobb, R.C. 'La commission temporaire de Commune-Affranchie' (Lyon), reprinted in **105**.

133 Cobb, R.C. 'Quelques consequences sociales de la Révolution dans un milieu urbain' (Lille), reprinted in **105**.

134 Cobb, R.C. 'La ravitaillement des villes sous la Terreur', reprinted in **105**.

135 Lagasque, M. Th. 'Le personnel Terroriste Toulousain', *AHRF,* 1971.

136   Soboul, A. 'Une commune rurale pendant la Révolution' (Authieux, near Rouen), reprinted in **103**.

137   Aubert, G. 'La Révolution à Douai', *AHRF*, 1936.

On the terrorists, see **130** *above, ch xi,* **129**, *ch 3, and:*

138   Lucas, C. 'La brève carrière du terroriste Jean-Marie Lapalus', *AHRF*, 1968.

139   Hohl, C. *Un Agent du Comité de Sûreté Générale: Nicolas Guénot*, Paris, Bibliotheque Nationale, 1968.

140   Boucher, P. *Charles Cochon de Lapparent*, Paris, Picard, 1969.

On the difficult question of dechristianisation, see **104**, *vol. ii, ch. 6, and:*

141   Plongeron, B. *Conscience religieuse en Révolution,* Paris, Picard 1969.

142   Mathiez, A. 'L'argenterie des églises en l'an II', *AHRF*, 1925.

143   Soboul, A. 'Sentiment religieux et cultes populaires: saintes patriotiques et martyrs de la liberté', *AHRF*, 1957.

144   Cobb, R.C. 'Les débuts de la déchristianisation à Dieppe', *AHRF*, 1956.

145   Paillard, Y.G. 'Fanatiques et patriots dans le Puy-de-Dôme', *AHRF*, 1970.

On the 'Reign of Virtue' see:

146   Mathiez, A. 'La Terreur, instrument de politique sociale des Robespierristes', *AHRF*, 1928

147   Mathiez, A. *Études sur Robespierre*, Paris, Editions Sociales, 1958.

148   Cobban, A. 'The Fundamental Ideas of Robespierre', *English Historical Review,* 1948, reprinted in **29**.

149   Cobban, A. 'The political ideas of Maximilien Robespierre during the period of the Convention', *English Historical Review,* 1946; reprinted in **29**.

150   Soboul, A. 'Robespierre et les sociétés populaires', *AHRF*, 1958.

151   Soboul, A. 'Robespierre et la formation du gouvernement révolutionnaire', *Revue d'histoire moderne et contemporaine,* 1958.

152   Soboul, A. 'Classes populaires et Rousseauisme', *AHRF*, 1964, reprinted in **103**.

153   Soboul, A. 'Jean-Jacques Rousseau et le Jacobinisme' reprinted in **103**.

154   Theuriot, F., 'La conception robespierriste du bonheur', *AHRF*, 1968; see also the eleven articles on Saint-Just in *Ibid*, no. 183, 1966, and no. 191, 1968.

On the final phase of the Jacobin dictatorship see **124**, *ch. 6;* **127**, *ch. 15, and:*

155 Bienvenue, R. *The Fall of Robespierre: the Ninth of Thermidor,* Oxford University Press, paperback 1968.

156 Mathiez, A. 'La division des comités gouvernementaux à la veille du 9 thermidor', *Revue Historique,* 1915.

157 Mathiez, A. 'La réorganisation du gouvernement révolutionnaire, germinal-floréal an II', *AHRF,* 1927.

158 Lefebvre, G. 'La rivalité du comité de salut public et du comité de sûreté générale', *Revue Historique,* 1931.

159 Lefebvre, G. 'Sur la loi du 22 prairial', *AHRF,* 1951, reprinted in **7**.

160 Rudé, G. and Soboul, A. 'Le maximum des salaries Parisiens et le 9 Thermidor', *AHRF,* 1954, reprinted in **103**.

On the Thermidorian reaction and the White Terror, see **25**, *book ii;* **106**, *section ii, part 2, and:*

161 Woronoff, D. *La République bourgeoise: de Thermidor à Brumaire 1794-1799,* Paris, Seuil, 1972.

162 Lefebvre, G. *The Thermidorians* (1937), English translation, Routledge, 1965.

163 Lefebvre, G. *The Directory* (1937), English translation, Routledge, 1965.

164 Tönnesson, K. *La Défaite des Sans-Culottes,* Oslo and Paris, Clavreuil, 1959.

165 Schlumberger, M. 'La réaction thermidorienne à Toulouse', *AHRF,* 1971.

166 Woloch, I. *Jacobin Legacy: the democratic movement under the Directory,* Princeton University Press, 1971.

167 Talmon, J.L. *The Origins of Totalitarian Democracy,* Secker & Warburg, 1952; Mercury paperback 1961; argues that the French Revolution was not so much a process of liberation as the origin of mass tyranny.

Among the numerous biographies of the Jacobin leaders are:

168 Thompson, J.M. *Robespierre,* 2 vols, Blackwell, 1935.

169 Walter, G. *Robespierre,* Paris, Gallimard, 1946.

170 Bouloiseau, M. *Robespierre, 'Que Sais-je?',* Paris P.U.F., 1956, 1961.

171 'Robespierre', special number of *AHRF,* 1958.

172 Carr, J.L. *Robespierre,* Constable, 1972.

173 Brunn, G. *Saint-Just,* Houghton Mifflin, 1932, Archon Books, 1966.

174 Gottschalk, L. *Jean-Paul Marat,* Chicago University Press, 1927, 1967.
175 Gershoy, L. *Bertrand Barère,* Princeton University Press, 1962.
176 Reinhard, M. *Le Grand Carnot,* Paris, P.U.F., 2 vols, 1950, 1952.

For the effects of the Revolution on the nobility, see:
177 Forster, R. 'The survival of the nobility during the French Revolution', *Past and Present,* xxxvii, 1967.

For a convincing demonstration of the adverse effects of the Revolution on the poor, see:
178 Forrest, A. .'The conditions of the poor in Revolutionary Bordeaux', *Past and Present,* lix, 1973; see also 131, ch. 11.

Two recent important publications are:
179 Patrick, A. *The Men of the First Republic: Political Alignments in the National Convention of 1792,* John Hopkins University Press, 1972.
180 Lucas, C. 'Nobles, bourgeois and the origins of the French Revolution', *Past and Present,* 60, 1973.

Useful taped discussions are:
181 (a) Johnson, Douglas and Hutt, Maurice *The Origins of the French Revolution* and *The Development of the French Revolution,* (Audio Learning Ltd., 84 Queensway, London W2.)
(b) Cobb, Richard and Hampson, Norman *The Crisis 1789-94* and *Personalities and Effects,* Sussex tapes No. HE12 (E.P. Ltd, East Ardesley, Wakefield WF3 2JN).

Index

149